Takht-i-Suleiman (Throne of Solomon) in Azerbaijan was first occupied in the 5th century BC. It includes a fortified citadel, the remains of a Zoroastrian sanctuary and an Anahita Temple from the Sasanian era (AD 224 – 651). The sanctuary housed one of the most important sacred fires in Iran. The Sasanian kings visited the fire altar before coronation, as well as before engaging in major battles. The citadel was destroyed several times and was partially rebuilt during the Mongol period in the 13th century AD. The site is recognized as a World Heritage Site.

Following page: Originally from central Asia, "Scarfaces" are demons representing hostile forces of the underworld; they were silenced and controlled by a slash across the right cheek. (Iran, c. 2000 BC)

Toy animals, hedgehog and lion on wheels discovered at the temple of Inshushinak. These may also have been used as offerings to temples as well. (Susa, c. 1000 BC)

ANCIENT IRAN

Massoume Price

ANAHITA PRODUCTIONS LTD.
Vancouver – Canada

ANAHITA PRODUCTIONS LTD.
Vancouver – Canada

CULTURE OF IRAN YOUTH SERIES

ANCIENT IRAN

Research & Text	Massoume Price
Project Director	Sheereen Price
Project Editor	The Vetter Group
Senior Editor	Joachim Waibel
Editor	Kirby Smith
Art Direction	Houman Sadr
	Babak Manavi
Production	Houman Sadr & Associates
	Babak Manavi
	Mehrdad Riazi
	Yeganeh Esfandiari
	Yasha Poursafar
	Malinda Dodds
Photography	Houman Sadr
	Davood Sadeghsa
	Joachim Waibel
	Afrooz Nasersharif
	Arash Mirlohi
Illustrator	Eliya Tahamtani

ISBN 978-0-9809714-0-8

DS254.75.P75 2008   j935   C2008-903743-X

Published in Canada by Anahita Productions Limited.

www.anahitaproductions.com

Anahita
PRODUCTIONS

Printed in Canada by Friesens

**This project is sponsored by Amid Naeini,
Joachim Waibel and Zohreh Waibel**

Contents

Opposite Page: Cart Wheel, Choga Zanbil (2000 – 1000 BC)
This Page: The Palace of Darius is one of the most elegantly built—yet strong—palaces in Persepolis.
Twelve columns supported the roof of the central hall from which three small stairways descend.
Figures on these stairways depict servants traversing the steps carrying animals and food to be served
at the king's tables. There are several carvings of Darius at this palace as well.

IRAN

Located in Asia and the Middle East, Iran borders many countries including Turkey, Iraq, Afghanistan and Pakistan, amongst others. There are close to 70 million Iranians, with 60 percent living in cities. It is estimated that around four million Iranians live outside the country. Iran has been home to many people from different ethnic origins, cultures, languages and religions since ancient times. Scientists, artists and educated people have developed large urban cities and extensive agriculture for thousands of years.

Iranian Groups & Languages

Iranians speak a variety of Semitic, Iranian, Armenian and Turkic languages. The group we call Iranians today arrived in Iran around 3700 years ago. At that time, they were represented by many different tribes, and were related to certain groups of people in India. That is why they are classified as Indo-Iranians. In ancient times, they spoke a number of different Iranian languages. The Baluchi, Kurdish, Luri and Persian languages that exist today came with these people. These latter languages are called Indo-European because they are related to many European languages, such as English. Today, 70 percent of the people in Iran speak an Iranian related language and close to 28 percent speak various Turkic languages. Iranian speakers of Semitic languages include Arabs and Assyrians; there are Armenian speakers as well.

Iranian Languages: Origins & Evolution

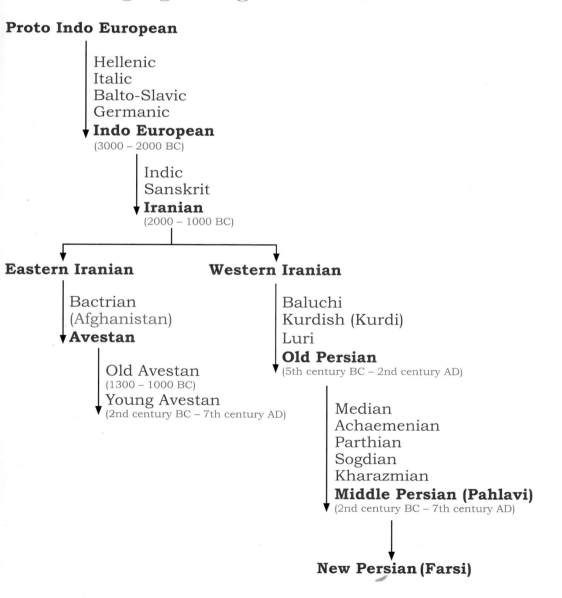

Proto Indo European

Hellenic
Italic
Balto-Slavic
Germanic
Indo European
(3000 – 2000 BC)

Indic
Sanskrit
Iranian
(2000 – 1000 BC)

Eastern Iranian   **Western Iranian**

Bactrian
(Afghanistan)
Avestan

Baluchi
Kurdish (Kurdi)
Luri
Old Persian
(5th century BC – 2nd century AD)

Old Avestan
(1300 – 1000 BC)
Young Avestan
(2nd century BC – 7th century AD)

Median
Achaemenian
Parthian
Sogdian
Kharazmian
Middle Persian (Pahlavi)
(2nd century BC – 7th century AD)

New Persian (Farsi)

Scripts

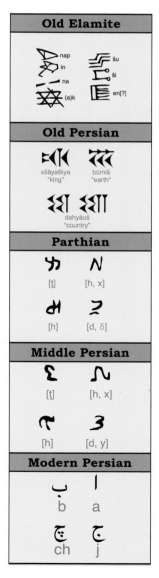

Old Elamite

nap
in
na
(a)k
šu
ši
en[?]

Old Persian

xšāyaθiya
"king"
būmiš
"earth"
dahyāuš
"country"

Parthian

[t]   [h, x]
[h]   [d, δ]

Middle Persian

[t]   [h, x]
[h]   [d, y]

Modern Persian

b   a
ch   j

5

The "Burnt City" & Beyond
3500 – 2000 BC

One of the oldest cities discovered in Iran is "Shahr Sookhteh"—the "Burnt City" in Sistan and Baluchistan, Eastern Iran. It is called "Sookhteh" (burnt) because it was destroyed by fire three times. This city is 5000 years old, and the people who lived there in ancient times grew crops, made pottery, wove beautiful coloured fabrics and invented interesting board games. The city is known for having made history's first artificial eye. Neither the language spoken by the people in this city nor its origin is known. However, unique inscriptions and signs exist, indicating that they had taken the first steps in inventing writing.

Above: The oldest textile fragments discovered in Iran are from the "Burnt City". This dyed, knitted fragment was probably made with a simple bronze knitting needle that was discovered nearby. (3000 BC)

Shaft-hole axe head with zoomorphic decoration (2400 – 1350 BC)

Excavations in the "Burnt City" indicate that pottery workshops were held outside the city to avoid pollution caused by burning furnaces.

This gilded eyeball was attached to the remains of a 5000 year-old skull. The capillaries show traces of gold, while the tomb suggests that a high-ranking female, very likely a priestess, was buried inside.

The Bronze Age is referred to a time when bronze was used extensively to make tools, weapons, and other decorative items. In Iran, it started in the 4th millennium BC. The earliest examples are from Susa and Luristan. Bronze (Luristan, 2000 BC)

Above: Accounting tokens were used for trade and to help clerks keep records of goods and materials. Five terracotta accounting tokens or calculi (Susa, 3300-3000 BC)

Right: Trade was extensive and to ease commerce, a standardized system of weights was developed. Weights in the form of a frog and the head of a bear (Susa, 2000 BC)

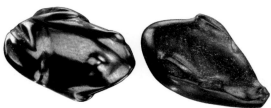

Below: Goat's Head Rhyton used for drinks during rituals and ceremonies. Ceramic (Azerbaijan, 3200 – 2100 BC)

Above: This game board, depicting a snake, is the oldest one discovered in Iran. It was buried in a tomb and indicates the belief that the deceased could continue to "live" after death.

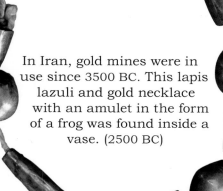

In Iran, gold mines were in use since 3500 BC. This lapis lazuli and gold necklace with an amulet in the form of a frog was found inside a vase. (2500 BC)

Mortars were used for mixing various ingredients and herbs. This small marble mortar was discovered near Damghan. (c. 3400 BC)

Elam & Susa
2000 – 1000 BC

Another beautiful and large ancient city was Susa (Shush) in southern Iran. Much is known about the people who lived in this area 4000 years ago. They were called Elamites, and today there is still a place in Iran called Elam. The unique Elamite writings have been transliterated by experts and the names of several of their kings, queens, gods and goddesses are known. Elamites played musical instruments like the lute, percussion and small string instruments, and they enjoyed dancing and singing. They left many beautiful figurines and statues, magnificent palaces and temples, and fantastic jewellery made from gold and silver–decorated with colourful stones and beads.

Ancient kitchens were often a corner of the courtyard. Cooking was done in clay ovens as well as over open fires. Wood was burnt as fuel, and charcoal was rare. Sieve, earthenware (1400 – 800 BC)

Glass bead necklace (Luristan, 2000 BC)

Ancient Elamites ate meat, fish and poultry. Grain was crushed and cooked as porridge or ground into flour and baked as unleavened bread. Fruits, oils, juices and honey were consumed regularly and barley was used to make beer. Beaker (2000 – 1000 BC)

Right: This ceremonial gold cup with mythical creatures and a sacred tree represents popular local mythologies. (Western Iran, 1000 – 800 BC)

By 7000 BC, small-scale agriculture was widespread in both Iran and the neighbouring areas. The earliest crops were flax, wheat, barley, peas, lentils and chickpeas. Flax was used in the production of nets, cloth, linseed oil and medicine: all had commercial value. (1st millenium BC)

Knob made of gold, copper alloy and iron (Northwest Iran, 1000 BC)

Animal sculpture discovered in Qazvin. (1000 BC)

Right: High-ranking women in ancient Elam enjoyed wealth and prestige. This life-size bronze and copper statue shows Queen Napir Asu. She wears an elaborately embroidered dress. The statue has an inscription in Elamite, cursing any one attempting to destroy the sculpture. (Susa, 13th century BC)

Strainer, red clay (1350 – 1000 BC)

Bronze was made from mixing tin and copper and involved mining and advanced smelting techniques. The manufacturing of bronze also engendered trade and import/export activity, since copper and tin mines normally do not occur in the same area.

Axe head (1350 – 1000 BC)

Spearhead (2000 – 1000 BC)

Beaker with ibex (Susa, 4000 BC)

Spouted jar (2000 – 1000 BC)

Funnel-shaped silver object (2000 – 1000 BC)

Bronze dagger
(3000 – 2000 BC)

Musicians and entertainers
were an integral part of palace,
temple and daily life.
Almost all categories of
instruments existed in Elam,
from clappers and scrapers
to rattles, flutes, clarinets,
oboes, trumpets, harps,
lyres and lutes, etc.
(Elam, 2000 BC)

Shallow bronze
bowl with Elamite
inscription (Arjan, Iran)

Earthenware bottle
(2000 – 1000 BC)

The Elamites used linen, flax, cotton and leather to
make clothing. Most households spun their own wool
and wove their own textiles. (Elam, 700 – 600 BC)

Chogha Zanbil Temple

Chogha Zanbil Ziggurat was built by King Untash-Napirisa (1275 – 1240 BC). This gigantic temple complex covers an area of over 11,000 m², with its highes tower reaching a height of 52 m. The inner walls had paved terraces on each floor, and the building contained an elaborate water treatment system. The outer wall had several gates; the inscription inside one indicates that the temple was built for the Elamite goddess, Lady of Lyan. It also housed a sanctuary for the deity Insusinak, the protector of Susa.

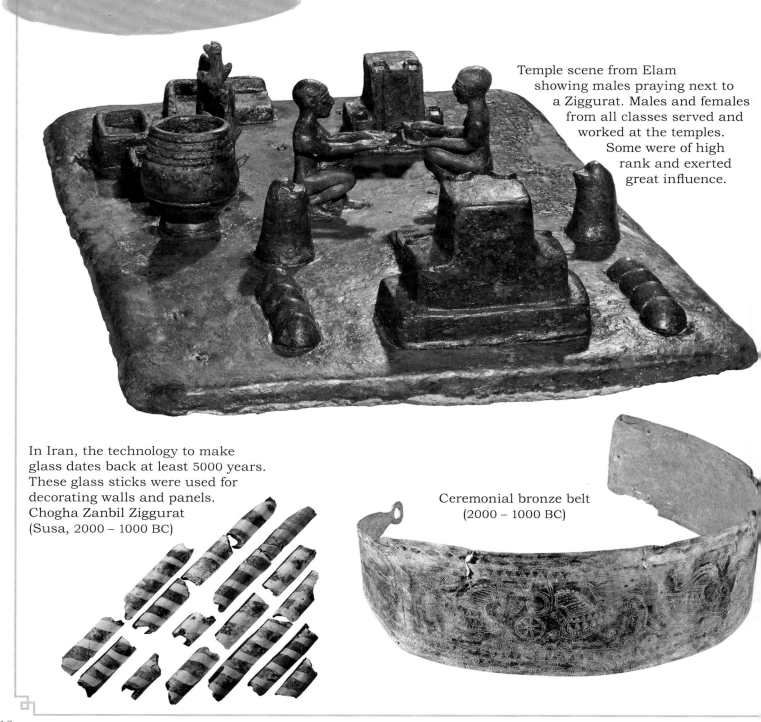

Temple scene from Elam showing males praying next to a Ziggurat. Males and females from all classes served and worked at the temples. Some were of high rank and exerted great influence.

In Iran, the technology to make glass dates back at least 5000 years. These glass sticks were used for decorating walls and panels. Chogha Zanbil Ziggurat (Susa, 2000 – 1000 BC)

Ceremonial bronze belt (2000 – 1000 BC)

The ancient Elamites worshipped several male and female deities and celebrated many joyful feasts with music, food and wine. Male worshipper making an animal offering to a deity or a temple. (Susa, 2000 BC)

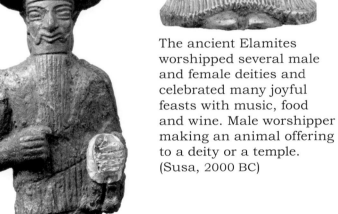

Male dignitary wearing a hat commonly associated with divinity. The pantheon of the Elamite gods was headed by the goddess Pinikir, the Mistress of Heaven. (Susa, 2000 BC)

Above: Goddesses and priestesses played a major role in Elamite cosmology. Many women including queens and princesses participated in temple functions. These images of an Elamite goddess dressed in sheepskin are from a ceremonial cup that was discovered in Northern Iran. (2100 BC)

The Medes
612 – 550 BC

Around 1700 BC, various nomadic tribes migrated to Iran over a period of 1000 years. These groups gradually occupied many areas in western Iran, and lived alongside other non-Iranians. The most famous of the Iranian tribes were the Medes and the Persians. The Medes formed the first major Iranian kingdom and managed to defeat the Assyrian kings of Mesopotamia in modern Iraq. Assyrian kings were powerful rulers and had forced thousands of Jews to come and live in Iran near Hamadan (ancient Ecbatana). The Jewish colony of Hamadan exists today and dates back nearly 2800 years. There is also an Assyrian Christian group in Iran that trace back their origins to ancient times.

In 612 BC the Medes defeated the Assyrians and conquered the legendary city of Nineveh. They united the Iranian tribes and started building up a new army with 3 main divisions: spearmen, bowmen and cavalry. (Medes, Persepolis)

Gold cup (Caspian region, 800 – 700 BC)

This decorative breastplate made of a thin sheet of gold would have been attached to leather and may have been fashioned specifically for ceremonial use or burial equipment. A breastplate shielded the chest from arrows or other weapons. The decoration on this example consists of mythical creatures, whose images were believed to provide magical protection for the wearer. (800 – 500 BC)

Gold cup (Caspian region, 800 – 700 BC)

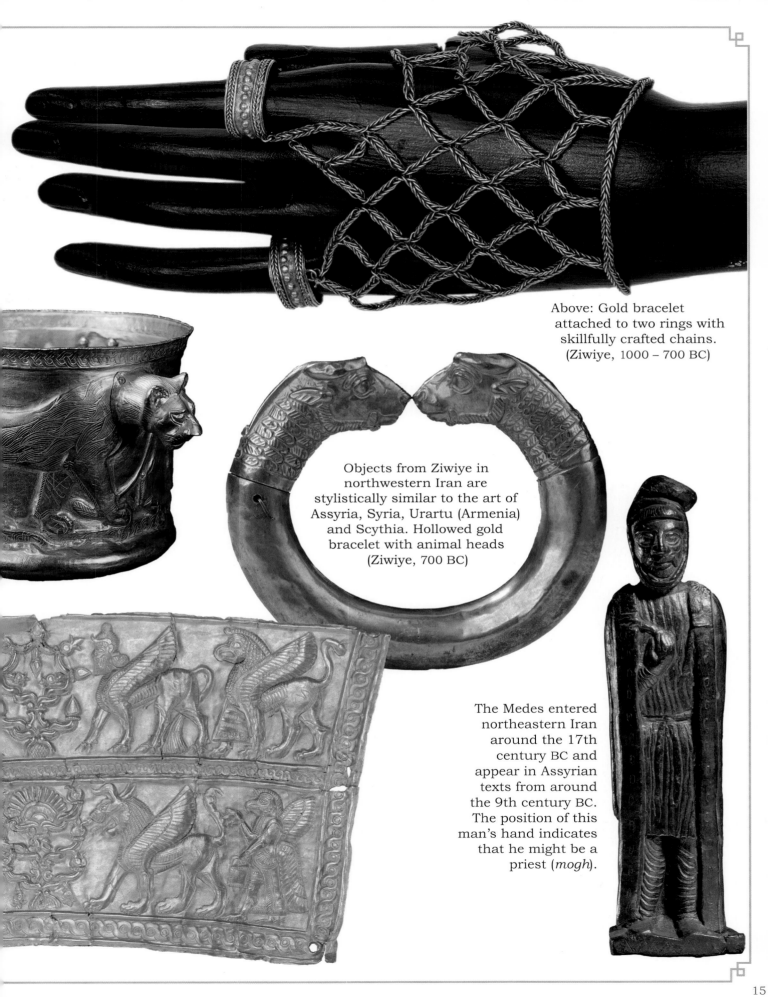

Above: Gold bracelet attached to two rings with skillfully crafted chains. (Ziwiye, 1000 – 700 BC)

Objects from Ziwiye in northwestern Iran are stylistically similar to the art of Assyria, Syria, Urartu (Armenia) and Scythia. Hollowed gold bracelet with animal heads (Ziwiye, 700 BC)

The Medes entered northeastern Iran around the 17th century BC and appear in Assyrian texts from around the 9th century BC. The position of this man's hand indicates that he might be a priest (*mogh*).

The Medes lived mostly in Hamadan and Azerbaijan, but gradually spread all over the region. They were known for their clothing and religion. Many wore tight trousers with tunics and long coats. They made trousers very fashionable and popular at a time when most men wore skirts. The priests, known as magi, sang important songs and performed prayers and other religious ceremonies for the royalty. According to the Bible, the Three Wise Men (Magi from Persia) traveled to the birthplace of Jesus to greet him guided by a comet. The Medes ruled for a short period before their close relatives, the Persians, replaced them in the 6th century BC.

Ancient Greek sources have made a number of references to the Median dress, particularly, the "Median Robe" worn by the Persian kings during ceremonies. Typical Median clothing included trousers and a tunic with a belt and hat. A long ceremonial coat with long false sleeves was worn on top. A similar coat is still worn today in Afghanistan.

Pressed gold plaques showing mythical characters were sewn onto clothing or belts. (Ziwiye, 7th century BC)

Right: Medes and Persians are often portrayed together in carvings at Persepolis. The Medes are mostly shown wearing rounded felt hats, different from those of the Persians. (Photo Joachim Waibel)

Left: Pins had multiple uses. They were worn in hair or with clothing and also had ceremonial and symbolic functions. (Luristan, 7th – 8th century BC)

Left: Median priest holding ceremonial branches. Gold plaque (Oxus treasure)

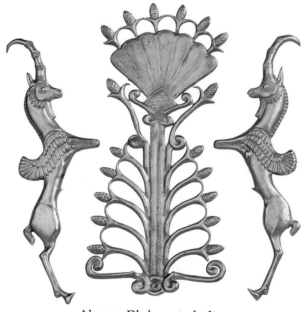

Above: Elaborate belts were a significant symbol of authority in Iran for many centuries. Leather belts were decorated with decorative golden objects. (1000 – 700 BC)

The Achaemenians
550 – 330 BC

The Persians were a powerful tribe and proved to be the most capable and efficient of all the Iranian groups. Kourosh Hakhamaneshi also known as Cyrus (r. 590 – 530 BC) founded his kingdom approximately 2500 years ago. He ruled over a small country called Anshan near the Persian Gulf. But soon thereafter he controlled a much larger region and managed to form the largest Empire the world had ever seen. He is remembered in the Hebrew Bible as a kind and generous man who freed the Jewish captives in Babylon, sending them back to their home in Israel to rebuild their ruined temple in Jerusalem. Cyrus became a legend and there are many stories about his life and achievements in ancient Greek books. He is best known for a piece of writing on a cylinder made of clay that is regarded by many Iranians to be a declaration of human rights.

Above: Cyrus the Great employed negotiation and tolerance to win political allies. This image is from Persepolis and is believed by some to represent Cyrus.

Below: With almost unlimited resources at their command, the Achaemenians were able to build monumental buildings to glorify their dynasty and assert their domination over the new empire. The tomb of Artaxerxes II (r. c. 436 – 358 BC) at Persepolis is one such example. Much of his wealth was spent on building projects including palaces at Ecbatana and fortifications in Susa.

Left: Discovered in Siberia, this textile fragment, decorated with fur and gold, is designed with a typical Achaemenian lion motif. (6th – 4th century BC)

Below: Gold daggers and swords were worn by the elite during ceremonies and official engagements, illustrating prestige and rank. (1000 - 600 BC)

Many spectacular gold objects from the Persian period show use of sophisticated filigree, cloisonné, repoussé and granulation techniques.

Built by Cyrus, Pasargad was the first capital of the Persian Empire. Currently, the only significant monument left is the tomb of Cyrus. He died in 530 BC while battling Queen Tomyris, the leader of the Massagetae, a Scythian kingdom. (Photo Joachim Waibel)

Above: Weight in form of a lion,
bronze (Susa, Achaemenian era)

Khavarnah, a winged creature, is believed to
represent the metaphysical power protecting
the kings and justifying their rule.
It may also be a representation
of the supreme god Ahuramazda.

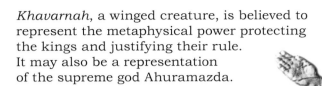

Above: These glazed kiln-fired bricks were
discovered at Susa and were used to decorate
walls and panels. (Achaemenian era)

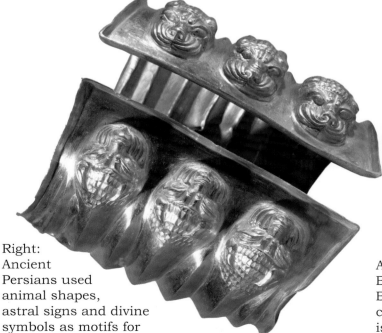

Right:
Ancient
Persians used
animal shapes,
astral signs and divine
symbols as motifs for
jewellery and luxury objects.

Above: In 539 BC, Cyrus entered the city of
Babylon. In this clay cylinder, now in the
British Museum, he describes his peaceful
conquest of the ancient city. This cylinder
is one of the most famous cuneiform texts
discovered.

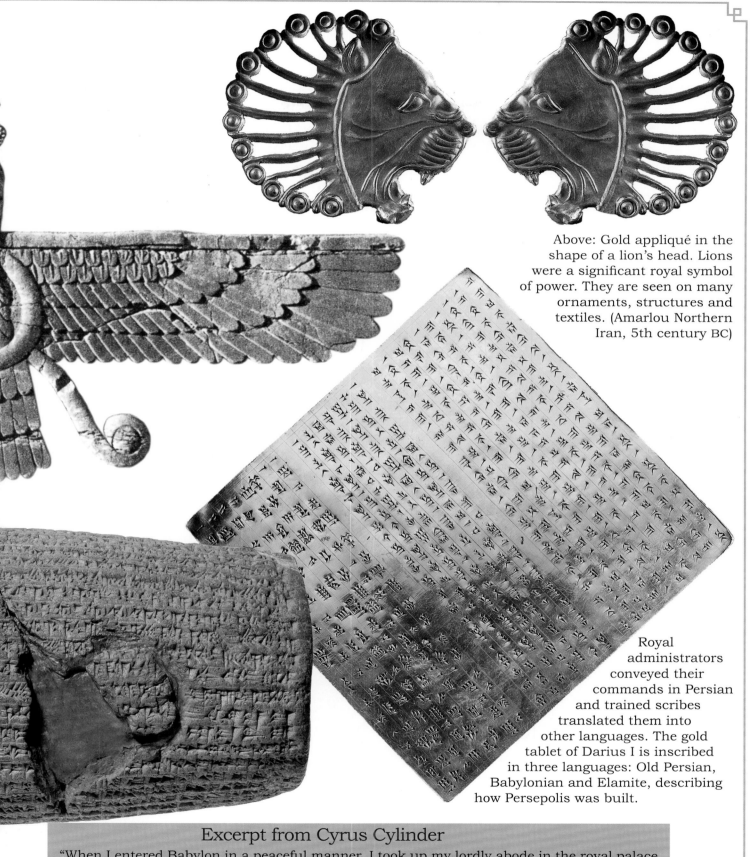

Above: Gold appliqué in the shape of a lion's head. Lions were a significant royal symbol of power. They are seen on many ornaments, structures and textiles. (Amarlou Northern Iran, 5th century BC)

Royal administrators conveyed their commands in Persian and trained scribes translated them into other languages. The gold tablet of Darius I is inscribed in three languages: Old Persian, Babylonian and Elamite, describing how Persepolis was built.

Excerpt from Cyrus Cylinder

"When I entered Babylon in a peaceful manner, I took up my lordly abode in the royal palace amidst rejoicing and happiness. My vast army marched into Babylon in peace; I did not permit anyone to frighten the people of Sumer and Akkad. I sought the welfare of the city of Babylon and all its sacred centers. As for the citizens of Babylon, Nabonidus imposed a corvée which was not the gods' wish and not befitting them, I relieved their wariness and freed them from their service."

Darius & Persepolis

The Persian Empire was further expanded and developed by Darius the Great (r. 522 – 486 BC). Darius built the magnificent Persepolis (*Takht-i Jamshid*) complex near Shiraz and celebrated the New Year (*No Ruz*) with dance, music, feasts, fires and prayers. The Persians ruled over many countries and brought together many cultures, languages and religions. They used three languages—Old Persian, Babylonian and Elamite—for running their affairs. Their empire was cosmopolitan, pluralistic and multicultural. People from different countries lived as neighbours, married each other and participated in each other's religions. One of the oldest Iranian groups, the Kurds, are mentioned by Xenophon in the documents from this period.

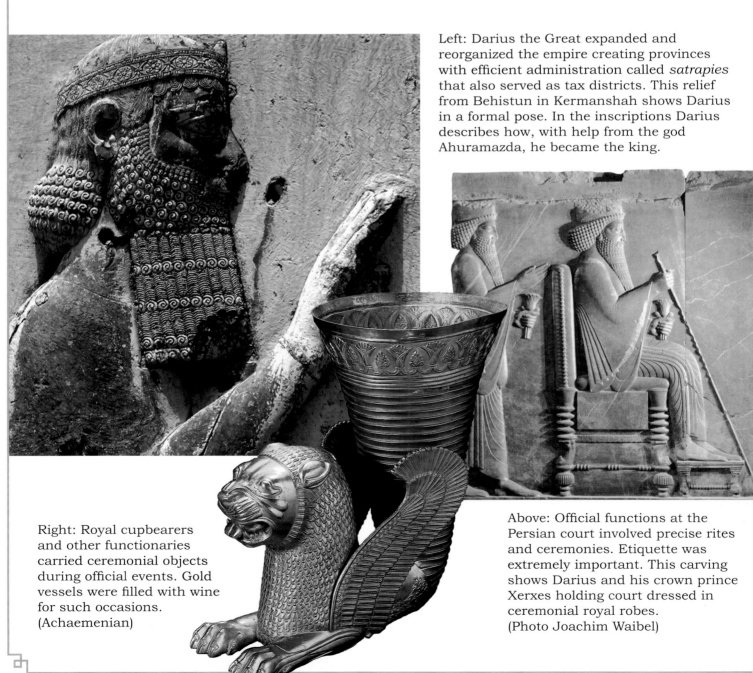

Left: Darius the Great expanded and reorganized the empire creating provinces with efficient administration called *satrapies* that also served as tax districts. This relief from Behistun in Kermanshah shows Darius in a formal pose. In the inscriptions Darius describes how, with help from the god Ahuramazda, he became the king.

Right: Royal cupbearers and other functionaries carried ceremonial objects during official events. Gold vessels were filled with wine for such occasions. (Achaemenian)

Above: Official functions at the Persian court involved precise rites and ceremonies. Etiquette was extremely important. This carving shows Darius and his crown prince Xerxes holding court dressed in ceremonial royal robes. (Photo Joachim Waibel)

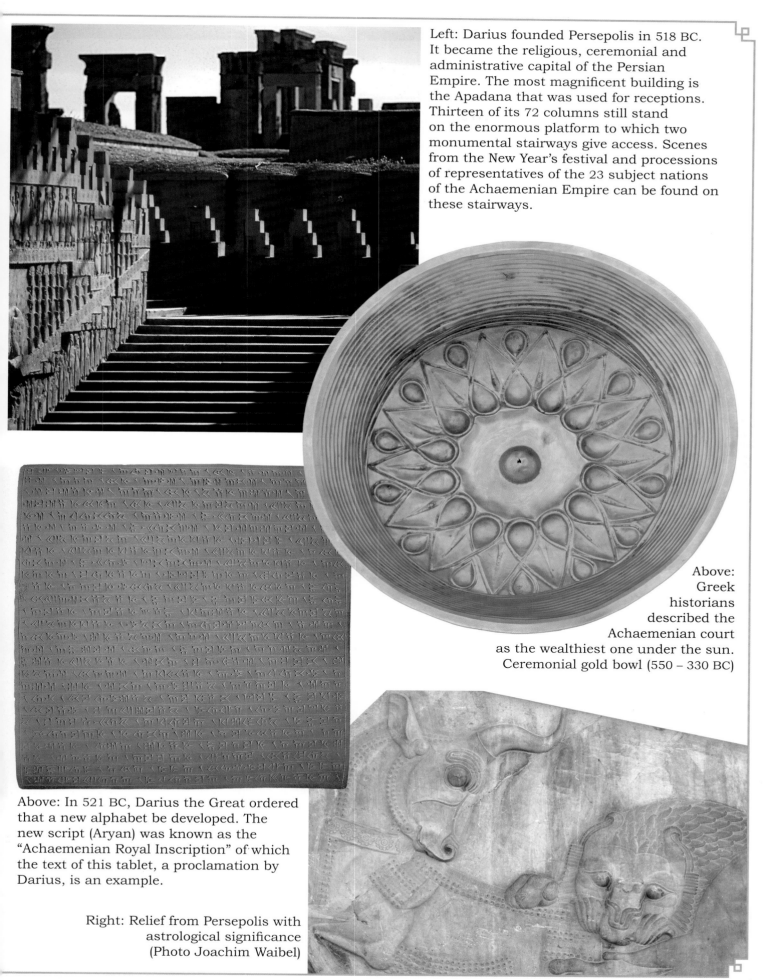

Left: Darius founded Persepolis in 518 BC. It became the religious, ceremonial and administrative capital of the Persian Empire. The most magnificent building is the Apadana that was used for receptions. Thirteen of its 72 columns still stand on the enormous platform to which two monumental stairways give access. Scenes from the New Year's festival and processions of representatives of the 23 subject nations of the Achaemenian Empire can be found on these stairways.

Above: Greek historians described the Achaemenian court as the wealthiest one under the sun. Ceremonial gold bowl (550 – 330 BC)

Above: In 521 BC, Darius the Great ordered that a new alphabet be developed. The new script (Aryan) was known as the "Achaemenian Royal Inscription" of which the text of this tablet, a proclamation by Darius, is an example.

Right: Relief from Persepolis with astrological significance (Photo Joachim Waibel)

The Persians built stable and secure roads, introduced the first postal stations to the known world and traded in technology, metals, foods, spices, gold, silver and luxury textiles like silk. The roads they built eventually became part of the legendary "Silk Road" that connected the Mediterranean and the Middle East to China. They hired the best scientists and physicians in the world and built libraries and astronomical towers for charting the stars. Darius' astronomer, Nabu-rimanni, studied lunar eclipses and arrived at calculations more accurate than those that Ptolemy and Copernicus were to arrive at over a thousand years later.

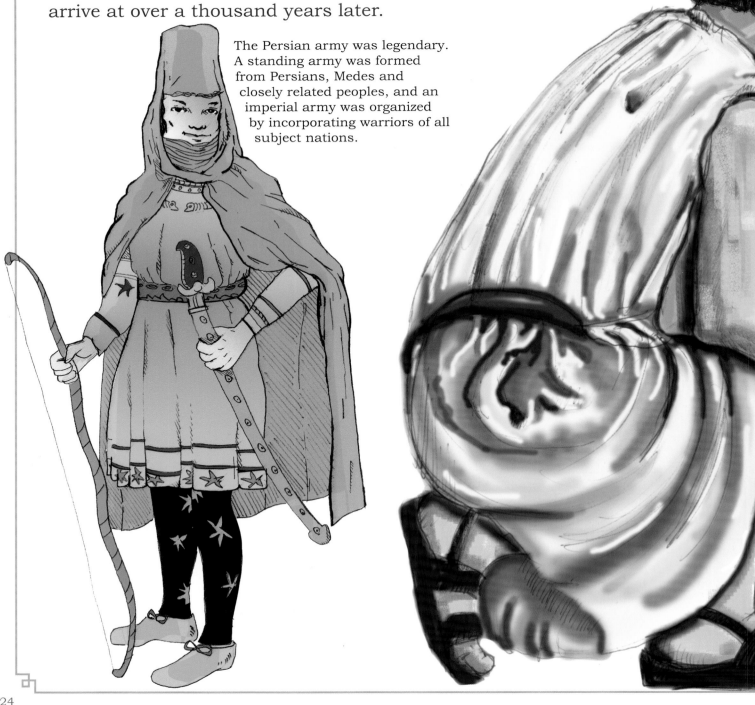

The Persian army was legendary. A standing army was formed from Persians, Medes and closely related peoples, and an imperial army was organized by incorporating warriors of all subject nations.

Below: Persian cities were cosmopolitan and regal. Inscriptions indicate that workmen were from every part of the vast empire, as were the materials and styles. Most workers were paid with rations and food, and were housed and protected.

The Persians created the first organized postal system. Secured roads had buildings at regular intervals where the carriers could rest and change horses.

Below: A popular symbol, the 12 petal rosette, was used for decorative purposes in architecture, jewellery and accessories.

Right: Tribute bearer offering tools as gifts to the king. Persepolis, audience hall of Darius I

Greek sources mention that the Persians treated their women with esteem. Mothers, for instance, enjoyed exceptional respect and affection. Nurseries existed for babies. The elite educated their sons and daughters, and children were taught never to lie and always to tell the truth. Persian boys were instructed to ride horses, hunt wild animals and fight. The records at the treasury and the archives in Persepolis show that women were able to work and to own homes and gardens. Sometimes women, as head of workshops, were paid more than the men who worked for them. Additionally, queens and princesses were powerful and wealthy, and had beautiful names like Parysatis, Atossa, Roxan and Mandane.

Above: Reading and writing was almost exclusive to the scribes who were trained at the palace workshops. (Photo Joachim Waibel)

Left: Ancient Persian society was male dominated. However, women had many freedoms, owned property and enjoyed employment opportunities. Enameled tile-relief of a guard from an Achaemenian palace in Susa. (5th century BC)

Above: Royal women exerted influence and had official titles. The king's mother was the highest-ranking woman in the empire. Many seals show royal women and their companions.

Right: Family was very important in ancient Persia. Persepolis archives indicate an extension of family terms where non-related people were called "sons" or "daughters" and the elderly were referred to as "father" or "mother" in order to express respect and affection. Head of a Prince in lapis lazuli (Persepolis, Achaemenian)

Artystone, wife of Darius I, and Parysatis, wife of Darius II (r. 423 – 404 BC), are mentioned in many documents as major landowners in Persia, Media, Babylonia and Syria. They traveled extensively and visited their estates with their own entourage. Fragment of saddle-cloth (Pazryryk, Achaemenian)

Right: One influential business-woman mentioned in the Persepolis archives is Irdabama. She managed her own workshops with several hundred workers of both sexes, owned properties and had her own private seal. (Achaemenian seal)

Looking Good

Persians wore beautiful, colourful clothes with shoes, boots and hats. Royal Persian gowns, worn by kings and seen at Persepolis, were decorated with gold thread and gold accessories. Clothes were made from wool, linen and cotton made at home, and from silk imported from China. Both men and women wore wigs and jewellery, and applied makeup. Minerals and herbs mixed with oils were applied to the face and eyeliner was made from kohl (*sormeh*) and lapis lazuli (*lajevard*). Perfumes were made from flowers and fragrant herbs. Women wore beautiful gowns, which were similar to the outfits worn by men. Kings and queens wore tiaras, earrings and bracelets decorated with turquoise (*firoozeh*) and lapis lazuli.

Left: Lapis lazuli has been used for cosmetics and paint for thousands of years. Persian legend says that the heavens owed their blue colour to a massive slab of Lapis Lazuli upon which the earth rested. Its use in Iran is documented from 4500 BC.

Gold bracelet with lion heads encrusted with lapis lazuli and torquoise, discovered in a royal tomb. (Susa, Achaemenian)

Gold griffin-headed armlet from the Oxus treasure. The bracelets are similar to objects being brought as tribute on reliefs at Persepolis. (Achaemenian)

Right: Clothing was made from wool, cotton, flax and silk. Royal workshops produced textiles for use in court and as gifts for dignitaries. Textiles were also received as tribute and for the payment of taxes.

Clothing represented rank and authority. Designs and colours were specific for different groups. Even the style of beards for royal males differed from those of other men as seen in reliefs of Xerxes and Darius at Persepolis.

Ancient Iranians left many personal items with the dead in burial chambers. These gold buttons with cloisonné and other ornaments were discovered in a lavish tomb. (Susa, Achaemenian)

Some Achaemenian-style jewellery has remained popular for centuries. Earrings similar to this pair are still worn today by some nomadic women in Iran.

The Achaemenians introduced their own unique attire. Silk was imported, while delicately dyed and embroidered cotton and wool were produced in large-scale workshops locally. Hats were made from leather, cloth and felt and were specific for different groups. (Photo Joachim Waibel)

Footwear was made from leather, felt, animal skin and cloth and included sandals, shoes and boots.

The homes of rich Persians were decorated with beautiful and colourful tiles and luxurious woven carpets. Persian carpets became famous during this period and were exported extensively. The wealthy used gold, silver and silks to decorate furniture. Tapestries were hung from walls and curtains covered windows. Bathrooms had hot water and small pools. Clay pipes brought water indoors. Soap was made from animal fats such as suet and herbs were used for aromatherapy. Persian gardens were lined with cypress and other trees, and were set with flowers, pools and running water. These gardens were called *pardis* and, to signify their beauty, the name entered Western languages as "Paradise."

Left: This young attendant from Persepolis is carved into the entrance to the king's private bathroom. He is carrying a towel and a perfume or oil jar.

Skillfully crafted furniture such as Darius' throne chair from Persepolis were made from exotic wood, decorated with gold leaf and covered with luxury textiles or leather. (Persepolis)

Left: Cypress trees are still grown in private gardens all over Iran. In ancient Persia they had aesthetic and symbolic significance and were probably associated with the afterlife. (Persepolis)

Right: The Pazyryk rug used as saddle-cloth discovered in Siberia is amongst the oldest in existence. It is identified as Achaemenian in origin. (500 BC)

Left: One of the important posts in the civil service hierarchy was that of the royal cupbearer. The famous Jewish scholar Nehemiah held the post during the reign of Artaxerxes I (r. 465 – 424 BC).

Ceramic tray with curved feet (550 – 330 BC)

Left: Spoons and forks and small sieves used for wine making are amongst many household utensils that have been discovered from the Achaemenian period.

Food & Drink

The archives at Persepolis provide some information on what the ancient Persians ate. They dined on roasted meat and birds, stuffed fruits and vegetables, olive oil, barley and wheat, and used a plethora of spices. Pistachio, pomegranate, peach, figs and grapes were abundant. Produced for almost 7000 years, beer and wine were widely consumed. Saffron was used in food and for making perfumes and makeup. For the wealthy, plates, spoons, forks and many other items were made from gold and silver; for others, simpler materials, such as wood, were utilized.

Right: The olive tree was one of the first plants to be cultivated. The practice spread from Central Persia and Mesopotamia to Egypt and Phoenicia and then to Greece.

Above: In ancient Persia saffron was used in cooking, as a ritual offering to deities, as a yellow dye, as a perfume and as a medicine. It was also dissolved in water with sandalwood to use as a body wash.

Above: Tributary offering gift to the king. Details from the east staircase from the Apadana Palace (Persepolis)

Above: Dates are believed to have originated around the Persian Gulf, and may have been cultivated as early as 6000 BC.

Servant carrying food or offering in a covered container.

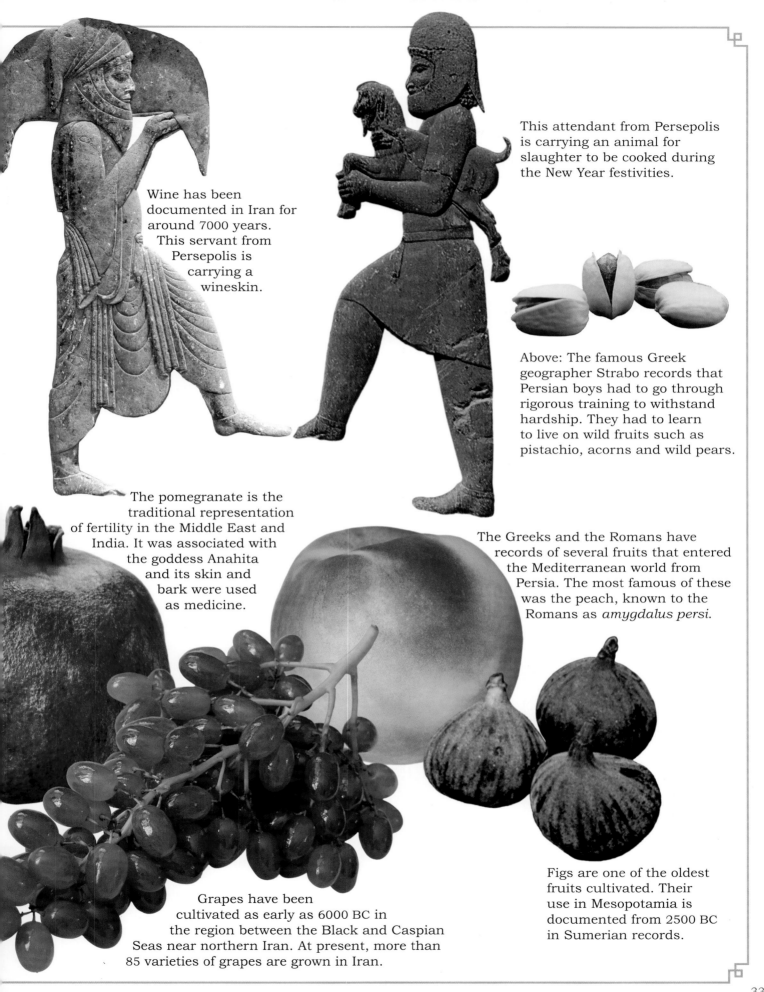

Wine has been documented in Iran for around 7000 years. This servant from Persepolis is carrying a wineskin.

This attendant from Persepolis is carrying an animal for slaughter to be cooked during the New Year festivities.

Above: The famous Greek geographer Strabo records that Persian boys had to go through rigorous training to withstand hardship. They had to learn to live on wild fruits such as pistachio, acorns and wild pears.

The pomegranate is the traditional representation of fertility in the Middle East and India. It was associated with the goddess Anahita and its skin and bark were used as medicine.

The Greeks and the Romans have records of several fruits that entered the Mediterranean world from Persia. The most famous of these was the peach, known to the Romans as *amygdalus persi*.

Figs are one of the oldest fruits cultivated. Their use in Mesopotamia is documented from 2500 BC in Sumerian records.

Grapes have been cultivated as early as 6000 BC in the region between the Black and Caspian Seas near northern Iran. At present, more than 85 varieties of grapes are grown in Iran.

The Sacred & the Divine

Ancient Persians believed in a God called Ahuramazda, meaning the "Wise Lord". Ahuramazda protected everything that was good and he was believed to be the wisest creature in the universe. Nature was respected and people were told to keep the soil and the waters clean. Fire was important and fire temples were built everywhere in the country, where people burnt incense such as wild rue (*esfand*). Anahita, a respected female deity, was the guardian of women and children and protected warriors during battles. In ancient times, she was portrayed with a lion and the sun. Eventually, the sun and the lion became a national symbol and would appear on Iranian flags until 1979.

Iranians were Zoroastrians. Other religions were tolerated and freedom of religion existed. Ancient Iranians participated not only in Zoroastrianism but in other religions as well. This gold model chariot shows two men wearing Median dress. The front of the chariot is decorated with the Egyptian God Bes, a popular protective deity. (Achaemenian, 5th – 4th century BC)

Religious functions such as burning incense or carrying sacred objects were part of the court ceremonies at Persepolis. The container above was used to carry charcoal during ceremonies and rituals.

Impression of a seal from the Hermitage Museum showing a king paying respect to Anahita. The cult of Anahita was introduced in the 4th century BC. An Indo-Iranian deity, she was called Aredvi Sura Anahita in the Avesta. She was associated with waters, healing, fertility and wisdom and remained the most important female deity until the Islamic conquest.

The wild rue incense (*esfand*) is still used in Iran to keep away the "evil eye." It is burnt in shallow containers during weddings and births, as well as at the New Year and in most festivities.

The Magi were an ancient Median tribe that specialized in performing religious ceremonies. The English words magician/magic are derived from "magi."

The oldest archaeological record for New Year (*No ruz*) festivities is from Persepolis. *No Ruz* was one of the most important festivals and was celebrated with grandeur. The wall carvings show the New Year procession with Darius seated on his throne receiving gifts from representatives of various subject nations. Babylonian delegation (Persepolis)

Alexander & the Seleucids
330 – 274 BC

The Persians and the Greeks were involved in many battles. Iranians ruled over many Greek cities and employed Greek mercenaries in their armies. The Persian Empire extended from Egypt to India, and the Persians ruled for 220 years until Alexander the Great conquered the vast empire. Once in Iran, the Greeks adopted many of the Iranian customs, married Iranian women and dressed like the Iranians. They also built Greek colonies and introduced Greek philosophy, theatre and arts into Iran. Ancient Greeks wrote extensively about Persia and the Persians and they popularized the name "Persia" in the west. Until very recently most Europeans referred to Iran as Persia.

Alexander's first victory over Persia was in 334 BC near the river Granicus in the northwest of what is now called Turkey. A year later he defeated the Persian king and ended the Achaemenian Empire.

In 481 BC, Xerxes (r. 485 – 465 BC) waged a major attack against Greece. To avoid sailing across the Hellespont with his vast army, Xerxes ordered a bridge to be built across it. Many boats were attached to each other and a road was built over the Hellespont Strait.

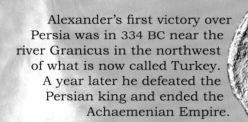

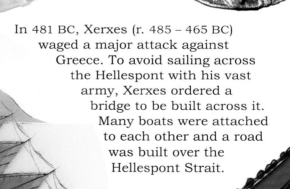

The Persian fleet during the Achaemenian period was substantial. In his famous tragedy, "The Persians," Aeschylus, who fought the Persians at Salamis describes the Persian fleet as consisting of 1000 triremes (battle ships popular in antiquity) in addition to 207 ships of exceptional speed. The first large-scale naval battle in which triremes participated was the Battle of Lade (494 BC) during the Ionian Revolt, where the Persian fleet defeated the combined fleets of the Greek Ionian cities. The model here is a reconstruction of a Persian trireme based on ancient descriptions.

Above: The Alexander Mosaic from Pompeii is a Roman copy of an earlier Hellenistic painting: it shows the battle of Issus. Greek historians mention that Alexander met and defeated the Persian army under Darius III (r. 380 – 330 BC) at Issus and then marched on to Persepolis. For four months Alexander lingered in the city. Before he left Persepolis to go in search of Darius, Alexander gave a great feast. It was then that the king, urged by the excited participants, allowed the palace to be burned. (2nd century BC)

Male head in silver (Seleucid)

Above: Silver coin showing Seleucus I. After Alexander's death his empire was divided between his generals. Selecus I inherited Asia Minor and Persia and founded the Seleucid Dynasty in 306 BC.

Greek occupation of Iran was brief. The next Iranian dynasty, the Parthians or Arsacid (*Ashkanians*), defeated the Greeks in the 3rd century BC. The Parthians were skilled archers and horsemen and ruled Iran for almost 500 years. They were so powerful that they managed to stop the legendary Roman armies from conquering Iran and reaching India. They traded with many nations and influenced the silk trade, which was of utmost importance to Rome. They were tolerant of other religions and allowed many Jewish and Christian refugees that were persecuted by the Romans to come to Iran and establish communities.

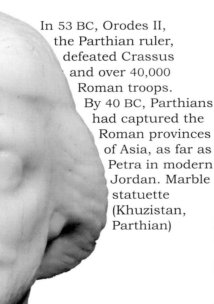

In 53 BC, Orodes II, the Parthian ruler, defeated Crassus and over 40,000 Roman troops. By 40 BC, Parthians had captured the Roman provinces of Asia, as far as Petra in modern Jordan. Marble statuette (Khuzistan, Parthian)

The elite Parthian women exerted great influence. This gold and carnelian seal ring shows a high-ranking husband and wife.

Parthians widely practiced Zoroastrianism, and gathered the holy texts of this religion. They also worshipped the cult of Mithra and contributed to the spread of Mithraism over the entire Roman Empire. Many Mithraic beliefs, practices and festivals were absorbed into Christianity and point to the influence of the Parthians on the ancient world. Standing man in Parthian attire (Khuzistan, 2nd century AD)

Parthian architecture was characterized by the use of sun-dried or kiln-baked bricks, with *iwan*, an open-fronted vaulted hall. The buildings were often covered with carved stucco reliefs and decorated with statues. Parthian rider, limestone relief (3rd century AD)

Parthians were master horsemen. The statue of the Prince of Shami (a region in Iran) shows tube-shaped leggings similar to full chaps worn on top of the trousers. The back of the legging is folded to make riding more comfortable.

Earring, or part of a diadem, in the form of a gazelle. The eyes are inlaid with carnelian beads, probably from the Caspian region. (Parthian)

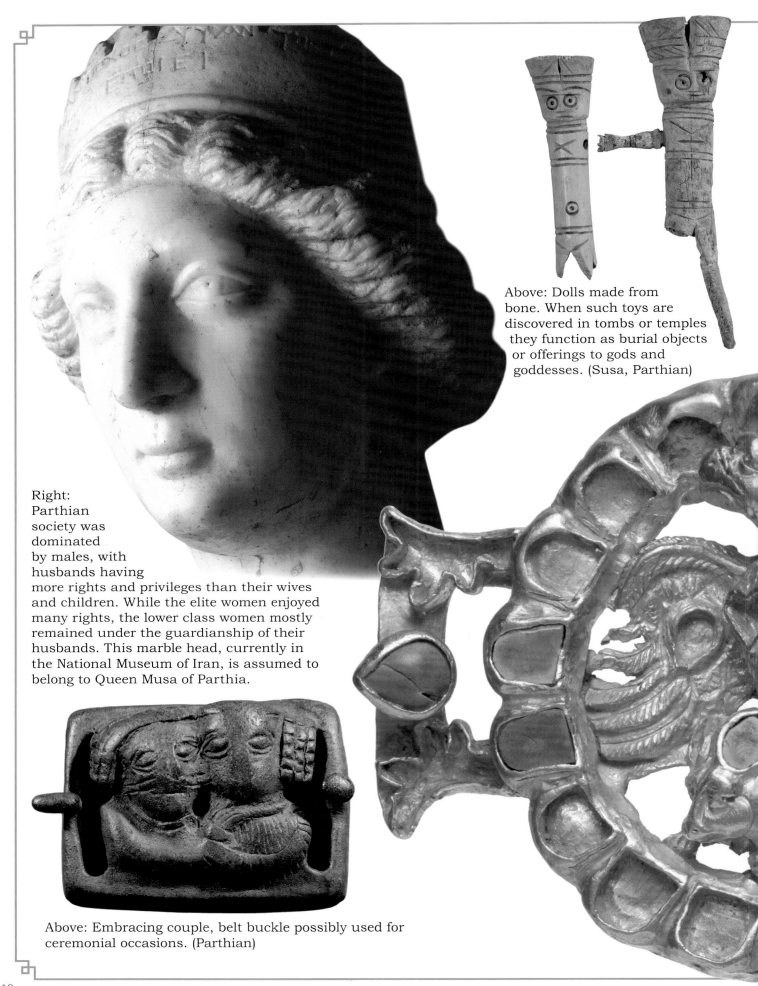

Above: Dolls made from bone. When such toys are discovered in tombs or temples they function as burial objects or offerings to gods and goddesses. (Susa, Parthian)

Right: Parthian society was dominated by males, with husbands having more rights and privileges than their wives and children. While the elite women enjoyed many rights, the lower class women mostly remained under the guardianship of their husbands. This marble head, currently in the National Museum of Iran, is assumed to belong to Queen Musa of Parthia.

Above: Embracing couple, belt buckle possibly used for ceremonial occasions. (Parthian)

Within the Parthian empire, trade extended from Syria to China. The Parthian military was responsible for the security and safety of the caravans. The task was awarded to local Parthian rulers with their own cavalry. Glass was produced throughout the Parthian empire and there is substantial evidence for the trade of glass with many other countries. Glass bowl with wave pattern from Jovain in Iran

Gold belt ornament (Parthian)

Gold necklace with semi-precious stones (Parthian)

Parthian Heritage

The Parthians were Zoroastrians and produced many copies of the ancient Zoroastrian text, known as *Avesta*, and built many temples to honour Anahita and Mithra, the patron saint of contract, truth and friendship. They were fond of literature and theatre and enjoyed entertainment known in modern Persian as *naghali*. Currently, it is still performed in Iran. *Naghals* were actors who entertained people by playing music and reciting popular stories and poetry. Some of their most popular stories appear in the famous storybook, "One Thousand and One Nights", which was recorded in Arabic hundreds of years after the stories were first told. The stories about the Iranian hero Rustam in *Shahnameh* and the medieval love story, *Vis and Ramin* also date back to this period.

Parthian is a North Western Iranian language. It was the state language of the Parthian Empire (together with Greek), and spread throughout Iran, Mesopotamia and Armenia, and was widely used in Central Asia. The oldest Parthian documents are from the 1st century BC. The Parthian script derived from Aramaic was written from right to left in horizontal lines. (Parthian)

The "Parthian shot" is a military cavalry tactic employed by Parthian mounted archers. The tactic consisted of a retreat at full speed and shooting at the pursuing enemy by turning their bodies. The maneuver required superb skills, since the rider's hands were occupied by the bow, where the horse was guided by virtue of the rider's legs.

Strabo, the famous geographer, records in 63 BC that the youth of Persia were taught music, and cites the use of elaborate martial music. Reverse of coin showing a harp

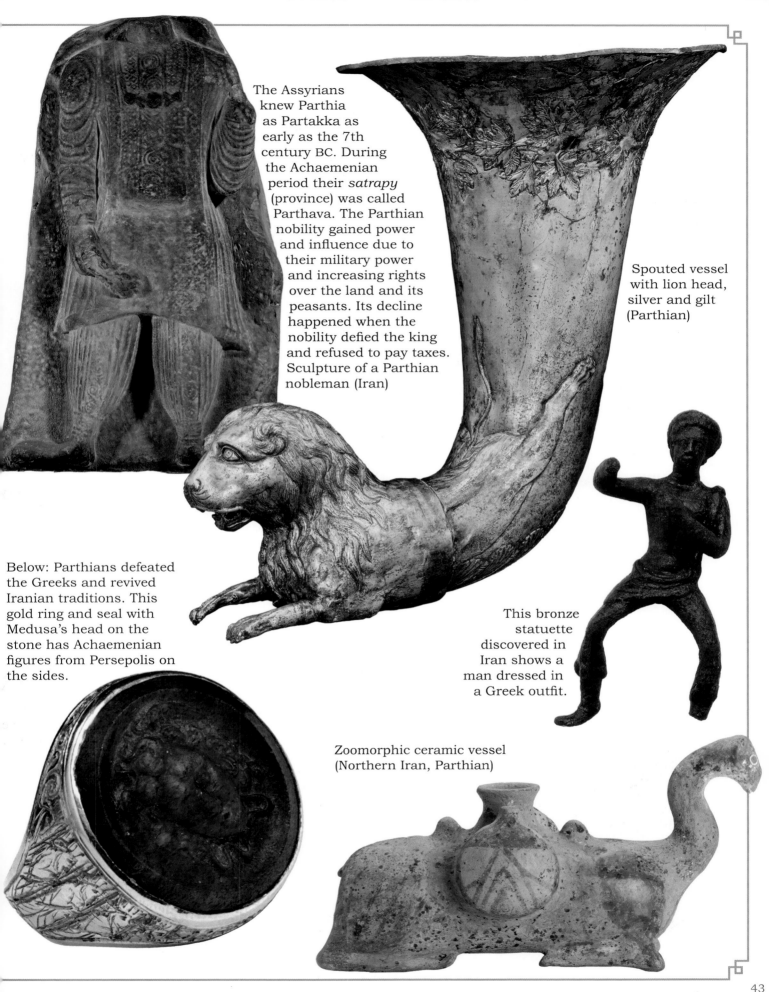

The Assyrians knew Parthia as Partakka as early as the 7th century BC. During the Achaemenian period their *satrapy* (province) was called Parthava. The Parthian nobility gained power and influence due to their military power and increasing rights over the land and its peasants. Its decline happened when the nobility defied the king and refused to pay taxes. Sculpture of a Parthian nobleman (Iran)

Spouted vessel with lion head, silver and gilt (Parthian)

Below: Parthians defeated the Greeks and revived Iranian traditions. This gold ring and seal with Medusa's head on the stone has Achaemenian figures from Persepolis on the sides.

This bronze statuette discovered in Iran shows a man dressed in a Greek outfit.

Zoomorphic ceramic vessel (Northern Iran, Parthian)

Parthians were famous for their beautiful fashion styles and clothing. Their loose-fitting trousers were popular everywhere and women wore beautiful dresses that, at times, resembled Roman styles. Belts (*kamar*), were a very important part of their ceremonial clothing, and both men and women wore headgear. Upper class women were powerful and sometimes those in royal marriages ruled with their husband kings as partners and lived lavish lives. Many of their popular names such as Geeve, Mehrdad and Ramin are still in use.

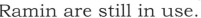

This elegant gold and turquoise necklace has four rows of delicately crafted gold chains, gold wires, glass paste and turquoise beads. (Iran, Parthian)

Parthians traded extensively in the ancient world. This glass bracelet is from Syria and was discovered in Iran. (1st century BC)

Left: In Syria, many gravestones depicting funerary banquets show strong Parthian influence with respect to clothing. Young man in a Parthian costume, holding a rhyton. Funeral relief from the side of a sarcophagus (Palmyra, Syria AD 200-250)

Gold earring with ruby (Parthian)

A subject of Parthia Queen Anzaze from the Kamnaskirid Dynasty ruled over the province of Elam with her husband Kamnaskires III. (80 – 62 BC)

Below: Originally a slave, Queen Musa (r. c. 20 BC – AD 4) was a gift from the Roman Emperor Augustus to the Parthian king Phraates IV. The ambitious queen reigned with both her husband and son as regent.

Below: Oils, fats and plant products such as resins and gum resins were scented to use as perfumes and stored in ceramic and glass jars. (2nd – 4th century BC)

The most spectacular examples of Parthian clothing are from Hatra, a border kingdom now in Iraq but under Parthian control in the 2nd century AD. There are many statues, created with great detail, of high-ranking males and females.

Parthian Bread

The most ancient recipe for bread in Iran is from the Parthian period and comes from Roman sources. Roman legions were familiar with "Parthian bread" and the Roman historian Pliny described it as the staple food of the Parthian soldiers and sailors. According to Pliny, Parthian bread was very hard, looked like a flat biscuit and "would keep for centuries" without going bad. Like other biscuits, it was baked twice to become drier and harder in order to improve its shelf-life.

Apicius: the Book of Ancient Roman Recipes

In the ancient book of the Roman cookery recipes, *Apicius*, compiled in the late 4th or early 5th century AD, several dishes are labeled as Parthian. They include recipes for lamb and chicken, a fish sauce and a dish made with beans. Here is one of the respective recipes:

Parthian Chicken or Pullum Parthicum

Apicius 6.9.2: Pullum Parthicum: pullum aperies a naui et in quadrato ornas. teres piper, ligusticum, carei modicum. suffunde liquamen. uino temperas. componis in Cumana pullum et condituram super pullum facies. laser et uinum interdas. dissolues et in pullum mittis simul et coques. piper aspersum inferes.

4 pieces chicken (breast or leg)
Ground black pepper
6 fl oz (3/4 Cup/170 ml) red wine
2 tablespoons (30 ml) garum (a fish sauce or substitute Vietnamese nuoc mam)
½ teaspoon laser (substitute asafetida powder or 5 drops asafetida tincture)
2 teaspoons chopped fresh lovage or celery leaf
2 teaspoons caraway seeds

Collection of spoons and forks (1st millenium BC)

Modern Directions for Cooking

Place the chicken in a casserole dish and sprinkle it liberally with pepper. Combine the wine, fish sauce and asafetida, add the celery and caraway seeds and pour the mixture over the chicken.

Cover and bake in a pre-heated oven at 375° F (190° C/gas mark 5) for 1 hour. Halfway through the cooking period, remove the lid to brown the chicken. Serve with some of the sauce poured over the meat.

(Adapted from *The Classical Cookbook* by Andrew Dalby www.parthia.com)

Fennel (Silphium); *Razianeh*
Silphium was in great demand in ancient Rome and had been imported from Africa, Iraq and Iran into Rome.

The oldest evidence for wine making in Iran is from the Haji Firuz mound (5400 – 5000 BC) in the northern Zagros Mountains of Iran. Several jars contained residue that has been identified as wine.

Caraway (Persian Cumin); *Faranbad* (*zireh*) These seeds have been used in food and for medicinal purposes in Iran since ancient times.

The Sasanians & *Eran Shahr*
AD 224 – 651

The Sasanians were local rulers of Fars in central Iran and the guardians of a major temple dedicated to the goddess Anahita. In the 3rd century AD, they defeated the Parthians, united the country, organized a national state and a powerful Zoroastrian church. They are known for their monumental buildings, dams, sciences, artwork, music, theatre and textiles. They built many new cities and created extensive irrigation systems for agriculture. They called their country *Eran Shahr*, meaning the country of Iran. By this time, around the 3rd century AD, the Iranian language was called Middle Persian or *Pahlavi*.

Right: The Anahita Temple at Kangavar in Iran was originally built during the Parthian era and was extensively reconstructed during the Sasanian period.

Left: The investiture of Khusrau II (r. AD 591-628) at Taq-i Bostan shows the king receiving symbols of power (*cydaris*) from Ahuramazda on the right and Anahita on the left. He captured Jerusalem in AD 614, taking with him part of the True Cross belonging to Jesus. His armies went on to invade Egypt and occupied Cyprus and Rhodes. As a result, the Romans attacked Iran. His successor, Ardeshir III (c. AD 620 – 630), made peace and the relic of the True Cross was restored to Jerusalem.

The investiture of the Sasanian kings involved elaborate ceremonies and rituals. Shapur I (r. AD 241 – 272) is depicted in carvings receiving the royal ring from the deity Ahuramazda (right). The horses are depicted as crushing defeated enemies. (Naqsh-i Rajab.)

Ardeshir I (r. AD 224 – 241) founded the Sasanian Dynasty and promoted Zoroastrianism.

Azargoshnasab Fire Temple in Azerbaijan was one of Iran's most important fire temples. A portion of the Holy Cross of Jesus that was captured after the victory over the Romans in AD 614 was kept at this temple and was taken back by force in AD 624 when the Romans attacked the city and plundered the temple. The sacred fire was burning constantly. An underground ceramic pipeline beneath the temple indicates that the fire might have been fueled by a natural gas source.

Gilded silver plate with dog-headed bird *simorg*. The mythical bird has a long history in Zoroastrian mythology and is associated with the spread of all seeds, healing and astrology. It was a popular motif and was portrayed on textiles and objects and has survived in the Islamic mystical literature of Iran. (Sasanian)

Stucco decoration was widely used from the Parthian until the early 20th century in all types of architecture in Iran. The designs show a rich mix of floral, animal and figural motifs, and some have religious symbolism. Relief (Dargaz, Khurasan)

Right: A pair of angels depicted at Taq-i Bostan resemble Nike, the Greek goddess of victory, and point to the extensive cultural exchange that existed between Iran and the Mediterranean world. (Kermanshah)

Sasanian Seal

There were centuries of wars between Iran and Rome. This Naqsh-i Rustam rock relief in Iran shows the defeated Roman Emperor Valerian and his ally, King Philip of Arabia in front of Shapur I.

The Sasanians made Ctesiphon, near Baghdad, their capital and transformed this old city into a major metropolis that included several circular cities expanding into the suburbs. When the Arabs destroyed the city in the 7th century AD, most of its bricks, marble and columns were later used to build a similar circular city that was called Baghdad, a Persian word meaning "God Given." At the time, the royal palace had one of the most precious and famous carpets in the world, along with many statues and paintings.

The Sasanian nobles were very wealthy and used gold and precious stones abundantly. This gold handle and chape from the 7th century AD was worn at battles and at official functions.

In AD 540, Khusrau I (r. AD 531 – 579) conquered the Roman city Antioch and moved many Romans to several new settlements near Ctesiphon. From this time forward the Arabs called Ctesiphon Al-Madain, meaning "The Cities."

Shapur I expanded the Sasanian Empire and fought the Roman Emperors Gordian III and Valerian.

Right: This large arch and sidewall are all that is left of the splendid city of Ctesiphon outside modern Baghdad. The arch is known as *Taq-i Kasra* (*Kasra's* arch). "*Kasra*" is Arabic for the Persian word *Khusrau* (King).

Right: Stucco wall decorations were popular with Sasanian architects. The images on this panel include animal figures and floral motifs.

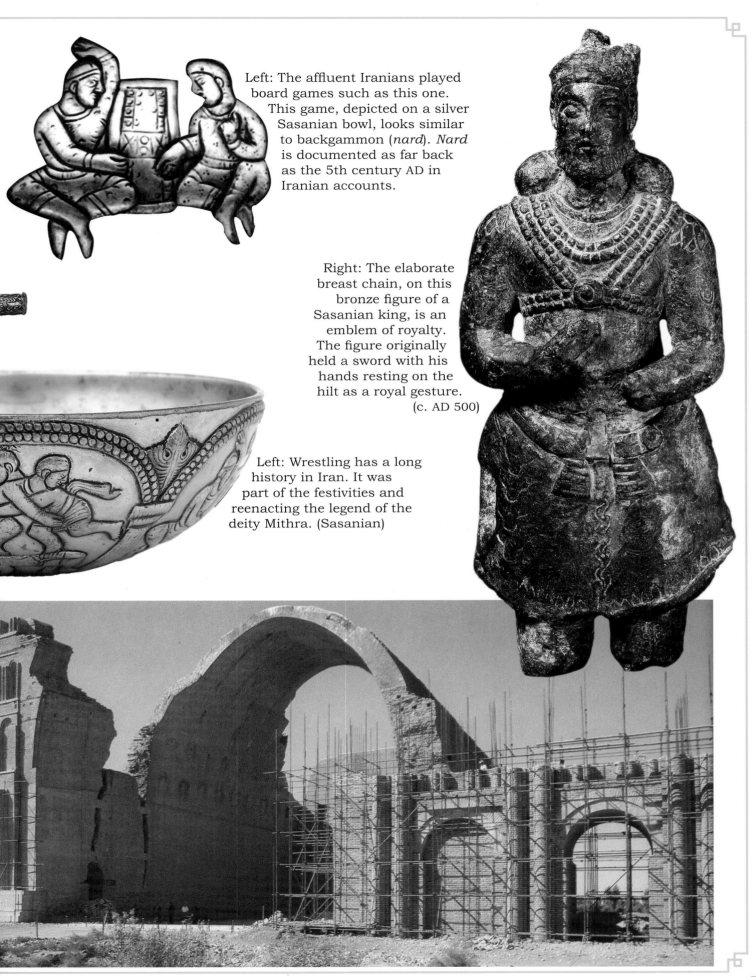

Left: The affluent Iranians played board games such as this one. This game, depicted on a silver Sasanian bowl, looks similar to backgammon (*nard*). *Nard* is documented as far back as the 5th century AD in Iranian accounts.

Right: The elaborate breast chain, on this bronze figure of a Sasanian king, is an emblem of royalty. The figure originally held a sword with his hands resting on the hilt as a royal gesture. (c. AD 500)

Left: Wrestling has a long history in Iran. It was part of the festivities and reenacting the legend of the deity Mithra. (Sasanian)

The Sasanians built an extensive library, a hospital and a university at Gundishapur in Khuzistan and hired translators from all over the world to translate books into Persian. One such book was the book of fables *Kalila* and *Dimna*, which contained stories about animals behaving like humans. This book was translated from the Indian book *Panchatantra* into Persian along with other Indian stories like *Sinbad Nameh*. Many stories have survived and been translated into many languages. Scientific and medical texts were also translated from Greek, Roman and Indian sources. Chemistry and physiology, for instance, were well known. Plants played an integral part in medicine and herbal remedies were prescribed along with mercury, antimony, arsenic, sulfur and animal fats.

The Sasanian imperial ideology was based on the assumption that Ahuramazda was the origin of all learning. Therefore, all knowledge was sacred. The library and the university at Gundishapur was the centre of learning with research and teaching facilities. Ardeshir I (Naqsh-i Rustam)

Right: Middle Persian (*Pahlavi*), both a language and a script, was the dominant script of the Sasanian Empire and was developed from the Aramaic script. It was in use from the 3rd century BC to the 9th century AD.

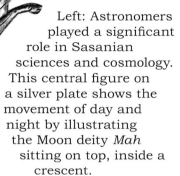

Left: Astronomers played a significant role in Sasanian sciences and cosmology. This central figure on a silver plate shows the movement of day and night by illustrating the Moon deity *Mah* sitting on top, inside a crescent.

Shapur II (r. AD 309 – 379) reigned during the golden age of the Sasanian Empire when science and arts reached their peak.

From the time of Khusrau I (Anushirvan) the Sasanian kings engaged in collecting and editing historical, scientific and religious texts from all the major civilizations. Sasanian coin with depictions of king and fire altar

The Sasanian imperial library was called the "House of Knowledge." Accounts of Iranian history and literature were transcribed and preserved at the library and qualified hired professionals worked to purchase, preserve, copy, illustrate, write and translate books.

The Sasanians were famous for their textiles, particularly their silks, and thousands of people worked in this industry. Their silks were exported all over the known world, from China to Europe. They supported art and their musicians made a lasting impact on Iran, Turkey, India, Spain and many Islamic countries. The names of some of their best musicians like Barbad, Nakisa and Azadeh (the harp player) are known from Islamic records. Poetry was also very important and in Sasanian times, poetry and music were so intertwined that most poetry was composed within a musical framework.

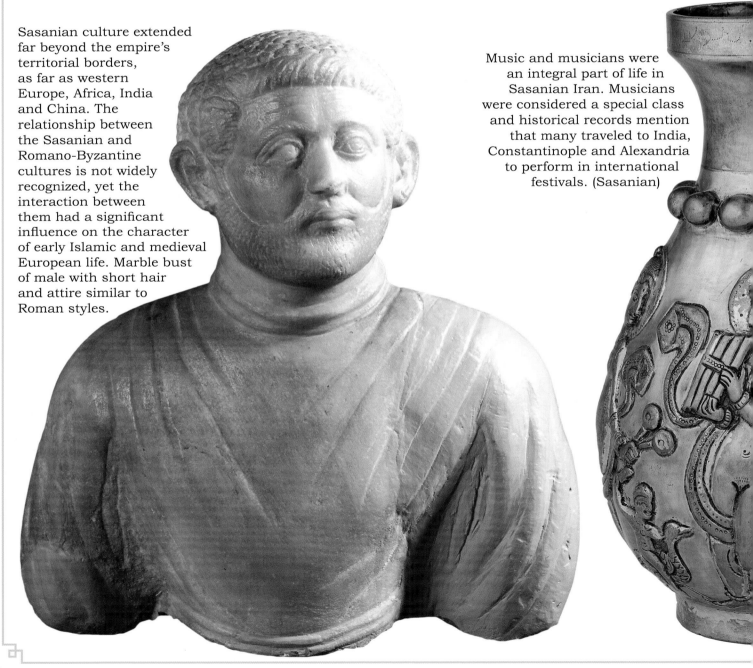

Sasanian culture extended far beyond the empire's territorial borders, as far as western Europe, Africa, India and China. The relationship between the Sasanian and Romano-Byzantine cultures is not widely recognized, yet the interaction between them had a significant influence on the character of early Islamic and medieval European life. Marble bust of male with short hair and attire similar to Roman styles.

Music and musicians were an integral part of life in Sasanian Iran. Musicians were considered a special class and historical records mention that many traveled to India, Constantinople and Alexandria to perform in international festivals. (Sasanian)

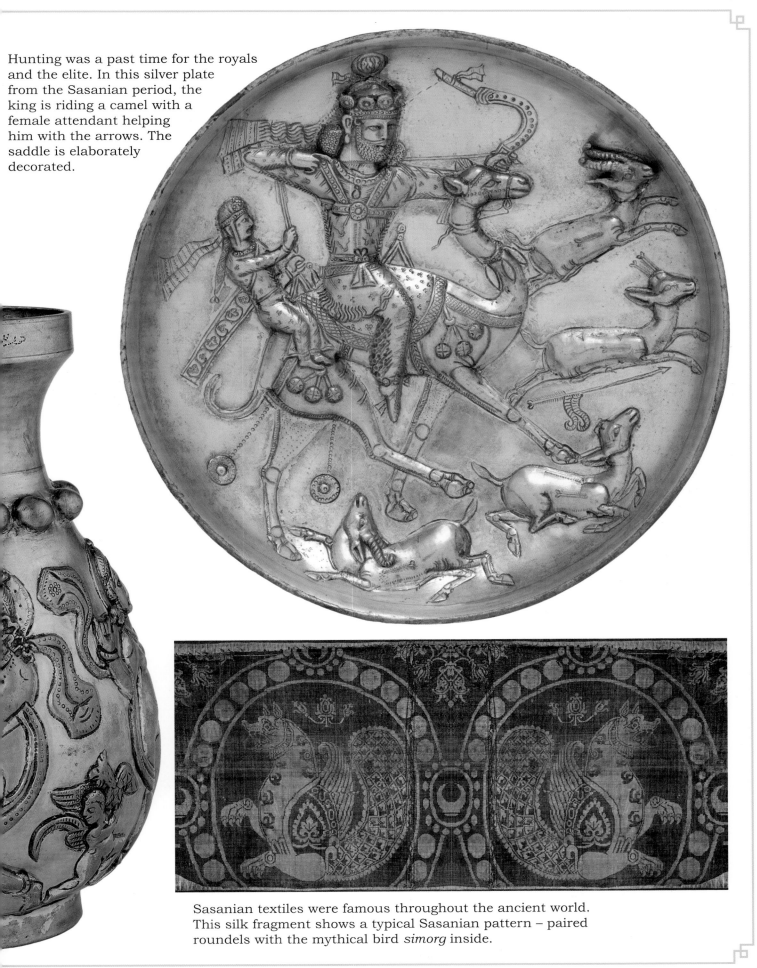

Hunting was a past time for the royals and the elite. In this silver plate from the Sasanian period, the king is riding a camel with a female attendant helping him with the arrows. The saddle is elaborately decorated.

Sasanian textiles were famous throughout the ancient world. This silk fragment shows a typical Sasanian pattern – paired roundels with the mythical bird *simorg* inside.

Women of Means

Ancient Iranian society was male dominated. However, elite women had many opportunities during this period. Two princesses, Buran-dokht and Azarm-dokht, became emperors and ruled Iran. They designated a "women's day" in the last month of each year. On this day women refrained from working and received presents from their husbands and family members. Their clothing and fashion styles were elegant and luxurious with beautiful designs. The most popular of the Sasanian designs were animal/bird figures, often depicted inside a series of small circles. For hundreds of years, artists from Egypt to Turkey, from Rome to Japan, copied this style.

Left: There is some evidence that in the Sasanian period, women attended school, at least for general religious studies, though probably in relatively small numbers. The main part of their training, however, consisted of domestic skills learned at home. There is also evidence suggesting that some women were well versed in Sasanian civil law. This seal belongs to Queen Denak (r. AD 224 – 241), the wife of Ardeshir Papakan, the founder of the Sasanian dynasty.

Right: This gold earring with pearl is from the Sasanian era. Jewellers used pearls, emeralds, rubies, turquoise and lapis lazuli while employing techniques such as filigree and cloisonné enamel. The techniques were similar to those used in ancient Hellenic, Roman, Parthian and Oriental jewellery.

Right: Sasanian queens shared power and prestige with their royal husbands. On this coin, Varhram II (r. AD 276 – 293) is portrayed with his queen and crown prince.

Above: Shapur I defeated the Romans in several battles and restored the borders of his Empire to those of the Achaemenian period. He founded the city of Bishapur in AD 266 to celebrate his victories and used Roman prisoners during the construction. He named the city Bishapur, meaning the city of Shapur. In this mosaic from Bishapur in Iran, a woman is wearing a long tunic with a shawl over her shoulder.

Left: Powerful royal women were commemorated with fires of their own. Adur-Anahid, the daughter of Shapur I, had the important title "Queen of Queens" and is mentioned before the king's sons in royal proclamations. This coin depicts Empress Buran and is dated AD 630.

The New Year (*No Ruz*) & other Joyous Festivals

During the Sasanian period the majority of Iranians were Zoroastrians, and gradually the Zoroastrian priests became very powerful. Thousands of temples were built and many rituals were performed at these temples. Zoroastrians regarded merriment and joy as religious obligations. They had many celebrations like *No ruz, Suri* Festival, Mihregan, Sadeh and Yalda, almost all dedicated to the forces of nature. At these festivals everyone came together and had parties where they sang and danced with music, drank wine and prayed for prosperity and safety. Modern Iranians still celebrate most of these festivals. Sasanians also loved games, clowns, and gymnastics, and made their national game, polo, popular amongst other nations. Today, polo is still played in Europe, North America, Australia, New Zealand, India and Pakistan.

Rock relief portraying a Sasanian king.

Anahita Temple, Bishapur

No Ruz: Celebration of Life

No Ruz means "new day" and is a celebration of the spring Equinox. It has been celebrated for almost 3000 years and is deeply rooted in the rituals and traditions of the ancient Iranian religion Zoroastrianism, particularly those from the Sasanian period. In the ancient Sasanian text *Bundahishn* (foundation of creation), it is said that the first seven creations were the sky, the ocean, the earth, the first plant, the first animal, the first human and fire/sun. Then, six holy immortals were created to protect these creations.

Three were male deities: *Shahrivar*, *Ordibehesht* and *Bahman*—protectors of the sky, fire and animals. The other three were female deities: *Khordad*, *Esfand* and *Amordad*—protectors of water, earth and plants. The concept of death did not exist in this perfect world until after the forces of evil (Ahriman) attacked it. The Wise Lord, Ahuramazda, the creator, sacrificed the first plant, the first animal and the first human; consequently, all remaining beings emerged and began fighting the forces of evil. Because of the triple sacrifices that Ahuramazda made, the sun moved for the first time, creating day, night and the seasons. This was the beginning of time, when the cycle of life (and death) began, and this day was called *No ruz*.

Sasanians celebrated it each year with grand feasts, music, dance, gift giving and, in the *Suri* Festival (prior to *No Ruz*), jumping over fires to celebrate the departed souls of their ancestors. Ahuramazda and the six immortals—whose names designate six of the months in the current Iranian calendar—were also celebrated, and are remembered in the ceremonial New Year spread (*Haft Sin*) tradition during today's *No Ruz* celebrations.

The Names of Iranian Months and Origins

The names of the Iranian months are taken from the ancient Zoroastrian texts, and represent the 12 major Zoroastrian deities venerated by the ancient Iranians.

MODERN PERSIAN	PAHLAVI	MEANING
Farvardin	Farvardin	glory of religion
Ordibehesht	Asha Vahishta	ultimate righteousness
Khordad	Haurvatat	health and wholeness
Tir	Tishtrya	the swift one
Mordad	Ameretat	immortal
Shahrivar	Khashtra Vairya	desired dominion
Mihr	Mithra	contract of friendship
Aban	Ap	water
Azar	Atar / Adur	fire
Day	Dadar	creator
Bahman	Vohu Manah	good purpose
Esfand (Espand)	Espandarmaz	holy devotion

Background: Sasanian plate with spring motif

The wealthy furnished their homes with all kinds of wooden and leather furniture gilded with gold. Cushions, carpets and wall hangings were colourful and sometimes were ornamented with gold thread and precious stones. The walls and ceilings were decorated with beautiful paintings showing legends, popular stories and famous people. Animal and floral designs made of stucco were also used for decorating buildings. Their gardens had large pools, lined trees and flowers, and they kept many different animals as pets. Their baths had cold and hot water pools with massages and aromatherapy provided by assistants.

Foreign dignitaries visiting Iran were impressed by the luxurious life of wealthy Iranians. Gold fork

Vessels with images of animals, such as the gazelle, had significant symbolism and were used in ceremonies, where they were often filled with a special liquid, probably wine. (4th century AD)

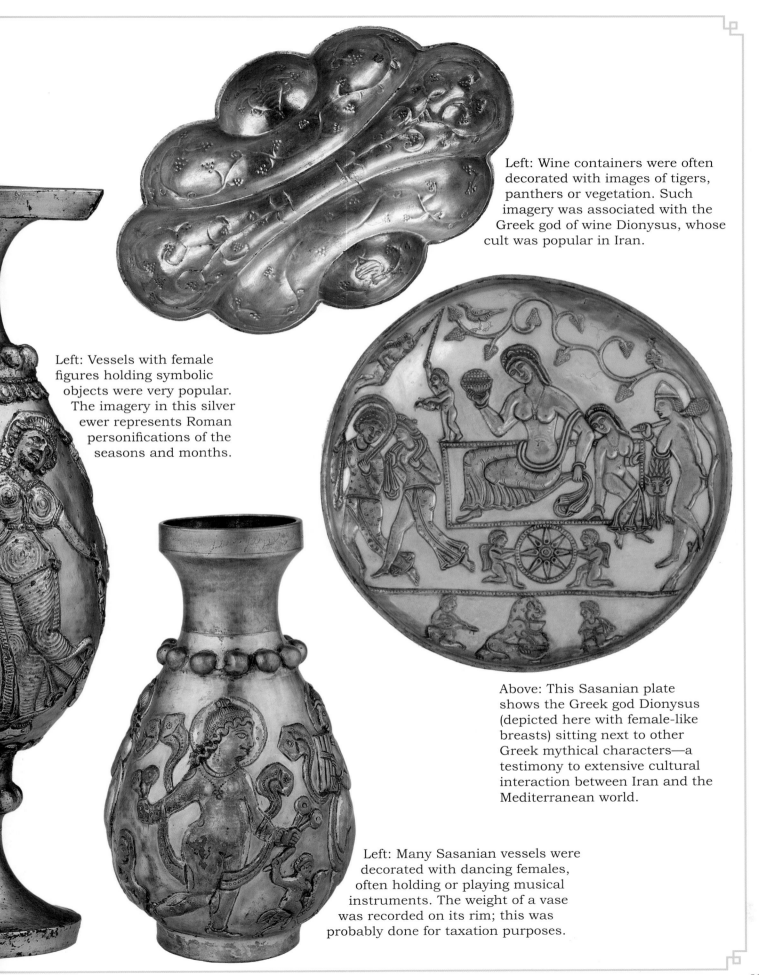

Left: Wine containers were often decorated with images of tigers, panthers or vegetation. Such imagery was associated with the Greek god of wine Dionysus, whose cult was popular in Iran.

Left: Vessels with female figures holding symbolic objects were very popular. The imagery in this silver ewer represents Roman personifications of the seasons and months.

Above: This Sasanian plate shows the Greek god Dionysus (depicted here with female-like breasts) sitting next to other Greek mythical characters—a testimony to extensive cultural interaction between Iran and the Mediterranean world.

Left: Many Sasanian vessels were decorated with dancing females, often holding or playing musical instruments. The weight of a vase was recorded on its rim; this was probably done for taxation purposes.

A Diverse Nation

The Sasanians ruled for almost 450 years. Kurds, Baluchi, Arabs, Gilaki, Tabari, Daylami, Medes, Persians and many others lived globally in cities and in new agricultural centers built by the Sasanians. There were many religions in Iran. Different Christian groups like Assyrians and Armenians, Jews, Buddhists, Manichean and Mazdakites practiced their religions, but sometimes faced restrictions and were persecuted. Their Empire collapsed when Arab Muslims attacked Iran in the 7th century AD. Their victory resulted in the Arab occupation of Iran, and major political, geographical and cultural changes.

Right: Shapur II hunting, produced in imperial workshops, such plates were given as official gifts to high-ranking individuals. Silver and gilt plate (4th century AD)

Above: This coin shows the goddess Anahita. She is often portrayed with kings during their coronation. Her name means the "Immaculate One."

Left: Wealthy Iranians used gold abundantly. Decorative gold objects were sewn to clothing and belts, which were also adorned with precious stones.

Left: Kartir (AD 241 – 272), the Zoroastrian high priest, was instrumental in creating a powerful, centralized Zoroastrian church at the expense of adherents of other religions. In this inscription he describes how Christians, Jews, Buddhists and Manicheans suffered great setbacks because of his actions.

Right: Qareh Kelisa (Black Church) was built between the 4th and 6th centuries AD, over the mausoleum of Saint Tatavoos, an apostle who achieved martyrdom by the order of the king of Armenia, in AD 48, for advocating Christianity. Armenians believe that the original church is the first built under the order of Christian apostles. (Azarbaijan)

Right: Shapur II receives a *cydaris* ring and a diadem common representations of royal power from the supreme god Ahuramazda. During his reign, the Sasanian empire witnessed prosperity and expansion.

Left: Silver and gilt bowl showing scenes from the life of nobility, celebrating a marriage. The upper classes played board games, were entertained by musicians and wrestled for fun. (7th century AD)

Time Line of Iranian History & Art

Pre-pottery Neolithic
8000 – 7500 BC

Agricultural communities are formed in western Iran. The earliest domestication of sheep and goats occurs at Ali Kosh in southwestern Iran. Clay vessels and modeled human and animal terracotta figurines are produced at Ganj Dareh in western Iran.

Pottery Neolithic
7500 – 5000 BC

Painted pottery and figurines from Haji Firuz show influences from Mesopotamia, indicating trade and contact with distant settlements. Neolithic villages in Tureng Tepe and Susian show use of domesticated animals, agriculture and extensive hunting. The size of the settlements grows by the end of the 5th millennium BC.

Chalcolithic
5000 – 3500 BC
Copper Age

Mud bricks (*khesht*) are used for construction. Villages have water storage and houses use their own cooking stoves. The number of villages in close proximity to each other increases. Tepe Sialk, Giyan, Jaffarabad, Djowi and Shahr Sookhteh and Jiroft are amongst the sites from this period that have been excavated. Susa is founded as a settlement and its graves contain many fine handmade vessels demonstrating diversity and skill.

Middle Elamite period
1500 – 1000 BC
Iron Age I

King Untash-Napirisa builds a new capital and a ziggurat at Chogha Zanbil in southern Iran. Glazed blue and green terracotta, glass and ivory mosaics were used to decorate the exterior and interior of the ziggurat. A stone stele of the king and an extraordinary life-size copper statue of his wife, Queen Napir-Asu, have survived.

Neo-Elamite period
1000 – 539 BC
Iron Age II

The inhabitants of the Marlik region in northern Iran near the Caspian Sea build cemeteries that contain rich tombs with precious metal vessels, glass objects and distinctive ceramics in the shape of humped bulls. Around the same time at Susa, molded bricks—some depicting bull-men and palm trees—are used for architectural decoration. Susa is expanded by the Shutrukid dynasty. The Elamites defeat the Kassite rulers of Babylon. As a result, Susa is later attacked and partially destroyed by Nebuchadnezzar I of Babylon.

Hassanlou Mound, near Mahabad, has produced a very important ceremonial golden cup with 3 gods of earth, water and sun placed on a carriage depicting a myth. (1200 – 900 BC)

Greek – Seleucid period
330 – 247 BC

Alexander of Macedon defeats Darius III and ends the Persian domination of the area. Upon Alexander's death, his successors divide the empire. Iran, Mesopotamia, and Syria fall under the rule of Seleucus I. Hellenistic art and culture emerge from a fusion of the various Near Eastern and classical Greek traditions.

Parthian period
247 BC – AD 224

Arsaces I founds the Parthian (Arsacid) dynasty. By 113 BC, Parthians control much of the former Seleucid Empire and move their capital from Iran to Ctesiphon on the Tigris in modern Iraq. The Roman legions under Crassus are defeated at the battle of Carrhae. A very distinct Iranian architectural style, *iwan*, an open-front vaulted hall is created by the Parthian master builders. Often covered with carved stucco reliefs, this form of architecture supplants Hellenistic styles in Iraq and Iran, and will play an important role in the mosque architecture of the later Islamic period. The new artistic style of frontality—where the head and body are shown frontally—arises in relief sculpture.

Mesopotamian period
3500 – 2700 BC
Bronze Age

The Iranian plateau is dominated and controlled by major Mesopotamian ruling groups, such as dynasties from Ur in ancient Sumer. The earliest tin-alloy bronzes are discovered in Susa and some ancient sites in Luristan and Mesopotamia, and date to the late 4th millennium BC.

Excavations at Cheshmeh Ali have resulted in the discovery of artifacts dating back to 7000 BC. Earthenware containers (5000 – 4000 BC)

Old Elamite period
2700 – 1500 BC

An Elamite dynasty from Shimashki, probably from Luristan in the central Zagros Mountains, overthrows the Third Dynasty of Ur and ends the Mesopotamian domination of Iran. Susa becomes a major city and the capital of the Elamite kingdom. Around 1900 BC, the powerful Sukkalmah dynasty takes control and establishes major agricultural centers by utilizing advanced irrigation systems. Vessels with abstract patterns, vegetal and architectural motifs, or naturalistic representations of animals or humans are made in southern Iran and are traded widely across the Near East from Syria to the Indus Valley. The earliest Elamite inscriptions appear around 2100 BC.

Median period
612 – 550 BC

From around the 9th century BC, the Medes are reported to be in the Iranian highlands and are regarded as threats to the Assyrian empire. By 612 BC, the Median king Cyaxares, with help from King Nabopolassar of Babylon, defeats Assyria. The following short-lived Median kingdom, with its capital at Ecbatana (modern Hamadan) in the Zagros Mountains, extends from northwestern Iran into Anatolia. Median artistic innovations are often regarded as the intermediary between previous art forms in the area and those of the Achaemenians.

Achaemenian period
550 – 330 BC

The Persian king Cyrus II (r. 590 – 530 BC) defeats Media, Lydia, and the Babylonian kingdoms, thereby forming the first major multicultural empire in human history. Under Darius I (r. 522 – 486 BC), the Achaemenian Empire extends from Greece and Egypt to Central Asia and India. The royal cities of Pasargad and Persepolis are built, and the newly constructed Persian Royal Road running from Sardis (in Anatolia) to Susa, facilitates trade, taxation, and communications.

Sasanian period
AD 224 – 651

Ardeshir I founds the Sasanian dynasty. Iranian imperial art reaches its peak. Although constantly at war, the Sasanians and Byzantines engage in cultural and artistic exchange. The use of frontality, introduced in the Parthian period, expands and becomes a hallmark of the Romano-Byzantine West. In the 3rd century AD, Shapur I expands the Sasanian Empire to its greatest size. Conflicts with Rome and Byzantium over the control of trade routes escalate. Domed square rooms are built with the aid of squinches (arched lintels) in the upper corners, a Sasanian innovation that influences Western medieval architecture. Shapur defeats emperors Gordian III and Valerian, and king Philip of Arabia. In the 6th century AD Khusrau I (Anushirvan) makes peace with the Byzantines and introduces a number of reforms. New forms of land survey and taxation

Sasanian relief, Dargaz, Khurasan

stimulate the economy. Khusrau creates four military zones, each commanded by one general. A new conflict with Byzantium lasts for close to twenty years and weakens both armies. A new city is built next to Ctesiphon. Caliph Umar ibn al-Khattab, from Arabia, defeats the Sasanian commander at the battle of Nihavand in AD 642. The last Sasanian emperor, Yazdegerd III, dies in AD 651 and Iran becomes part of the Arab-Muslim Empire.

Glossary

Achaemenian: The first major Iranian dynasty formed by the Persians. At their peak, their empire extended from India to Egypt. They ruled from 550 to 330 BC when Alexander the Great defeated their last king.

Ahriman: The name means the "Lord of Hostility" and it represents the spirit of evil in Zoroastrianism.

Ahuramazda: The supreme god of the ancient Persians, and the most important Iranian deity before Islam. His name means the "Wise Lord".

Alexander the Great (336 - 323 BC): The young Macedonian king who ended the Persian Empire. Alexander also invaded Egypt, Babylonia, Media, Bactria and the Valley of Indus.

Anahita: An ancient Iranian goddess, she is associated with water and fertility, and was a patron of women and warriors. Her name means the "Immaculate One". She was popularized by the Achaemenians, and remained an important deity with major temples until the conquest of Islam.

Aramaic: The language of many Semitic peoples throughout the ancient Near East. It was replaced by Arabic after the Muslim conquest. The Christians in Iraq, Iran, Syria, Turkey and Lebanon have maintained the Aramaic language.

Armenia (ancient Urartu): A region and ancient kingdom comprised of parts of Asia Minor (Turkey) and the Caucasus. Armenia was the first country to adopt Christianity in AD 301.

Assyria: Ancient name for the northeastern part of modern Iraq. It was one of the greatest empires of antiquity. Assyria was overthrown is 612 BC by the Medes and the Babylonians. Assyrians comprise a small Christian minority group in modern Iran, Turkey, Syria and Iraq.

Avesta: The sacred literature of the ancient and modern Zoroastrians. It is written in two dialects; Old and Younger Avestan.

Alexander the Great

Anahita

Azerbaijan: The ancient Iranian province of Atropatene, Azerbaijan occupies the southeastern part of the Caucasus, descending to the Caspian Sea, between Iran and Russia.

Babylonia: An ancient urban civilization in Mesopotamia (modern Iraq). It lasted from the 18th until the 6th century BC. Its capital, the legendary city of Babylon, became one of the major centers of the Achaemenian Empire.

Bactria: Located in northern Afghanistan, this ancient Greek kingdom was an eastern province of the Persian Empire before its conquest by Alexander.

Baluchi: An Iranian group and a language in Iran. The Baluchi live in Pakistan, eastern Iran (Baluchistan) and southern Afghanistan.

Daylami: An Iranian group inhabiting the ancient province of Daylam in northern Iran.

Elam: The coastal regions along the northern shore of the Persian Gulf, from what is now Kuwait to the Straits of Hurmuz. The ancient kingdom of Elam, with Susa as its capital, was one of the earliest urbanized centers in Iran, and has been inhabited extensively from 3300 BC.

Esfand: Wild rue, a stink plant with yellow flowers.

Fars (Parsua): The ancient province inhabited by Persians who gave their name to the area that comprises present day Fars.

Gilaki: An Iranian group living in the northern Iran–mainly the province of Gilan.

Haft Sin: The ceremonial spread for the Iranian New Year. It means seven 'S's and the spread contains seven items that start with the letter 'S' in addition to other items.

Khwarazm: An ancient Persian province, the area is located in present day Uzbekistan.

Kurdistan: A province in Iran, it contains both Turkish and Kurdish populations.

Kurds: An Iranian group living in Iran, Turkey, Iraq and parts of Russia, as well as Syria. They have two main languages belonging to the northwestern Iranian group of the Indo-European family of languages with many dialects.

Luristan: A province located in western Iran. The inhabitants are mainly Luri and Bakhtyari and the area has been home to many groups including ancient Kassites.

Lurs: An Indo-Iranian group, they occupy western and southwestern Iran and some still live as nomads. Sources as late as 16th century AD, identify them as a Kurdish tribe, speaking a Kurdish related language.

Manicheanism: A religion founded by the Persian Sage Mani in the latter half of the 3rd century AD. It aspired to be the true synthesis of the major religions at the time, and consisted of Zoroastrian dualism, Babylonian folklore, Buddhist ethics, and Christian/Jewish elements.

Massagetae: Belonging to the Saka nation, these ancient Scythians lived between the Caspian and Aral Seas. Cyrus the Great was killed battling them.

Mazdakites: Followers of a religious sect founded by the Iranian Sage, Mazdak in the 6th century AD. They believed that there were two original principles of the universe: Light (good) and Darkness (evil).

Medes: Ancient Indo-Iranian tribes who became the first Iranian rulers of both Mesopotamia and Iran, occupying parts of Azerbaijan, Kermanshah and Kurdistan.

Media: Ancient territory of northwestern Iran generally corresponding to the modern regions of Azerbaijan, Kurdistan and parts of Kermanshah.

Mesopotamia: The word means between two rivers, and the area is referred to the farmland located in a narrow strip of land between the Tigris and Euphrates rivers in present day Iraq. It is known as the cradle of civilization due to the emergence of the earliest urban civilizations in this area.

Middle Persian: Both a script and a language, it became the dominant script of the Sasanian Empire (AD 224 – 651), and was developed from the Aramaic script. The language derived from Old Persian, and was extensively in use from the 3rd century BC to the 9th century AD, before evolving into New Persian.

Mihregan Festival: The coming of seasons was celebrated by the ancient Iranians through *No Ruz* and Mihregan (Mitrakana). Dedicated to the deity Mihr (Mithra), originally, it has been an ancient harvest festival. It is celebrated by the modern Iranians to commemorate knowledge and learning and it coincides with the beginning of the school year.

Mithra (Mihr): An ancient Indo-Iranian deity, Mithra became a significant cult with major temples in Iran and Roman territories. In the Zoroastrian tradition, it was the deity protector of the covenant and of loyalty. In modern Persian it means love and kindness.

Modern Persian: Language spoken principally in Iran, Afghanistan and Tajikistan. Persian belongs to the Iranian branch of the Indo-European language.

No Ruz (New Year): The Iranian New Year is a celebration of spring equinox and has been celebrated since Achaemenian times from around 500 BC. It is Zoroastrian in origin and has been influenced by ancient Mesopotamian festivals, among others. Its current form is closely related to the New Year celebrations during the Sasanian period, 7th century AD. It is the most important national festival in Iran.

Mithra, Shapur II & Ahuramazda

Old Iranian: A sub-group of Indo-European languages which spread across the Iranian plateau (1350 – 350 BC). Of these languages, Avestan and Old Persian are textually preserved. Others such as Median, Parthian, Sogdian, Carduchi and Scythian are known from Greek sources.

Old Persian: Old Persian was spoken in southwestern Iran, and was contemporary to Avestan spoken in the northeast. The oldest traces of Old Persian date to the 6th century BC. It was spoken until the 3rd century BC, and is preserved in cuneiform tablets from Achaemenian dynasty.

Oxus Treasure: A large collection of gold and silver objects from the Achaemenian period discovered near the river Oxus. Most are in the British and Victoria and Albert museums in London.

Pahlavi: Both a language and a script. Pahlavi is an Iranian language spoken between the 3rd century BC and the 9th century AD. The Pahlavi script evolved from the Aramaic script and was written from right to left. The last Iranian dynasty in Iran adopted the same name in 20th century.

Parthia (Parthava): Belonging to the Parni tribe, these Iranian tribes moving south became known as Parthians, and created a major empire. They were settled in northwest Iran before expanding, and were praised for their archery and horsemanship.

Persepolis: The name means the city of Persians in Greek. Persepolis was the ceremonial capital of the Achaemenian Empire. It was built during the reign of Darius I, and developed further by successive kings. Its majestic audience halls and residential palaces perished in flames when Alexander the Great conquered and looted Persepolis in 330 BC.

Parthian

Persians: An Indo-Iranian group who entered western Iran around 1000 BC, conquered the entire area, and created the Persian Empire.

Sadeh Festival: Sadeh means 100, and is a mid-winter feast marking the 100 days before *No Ruz*. It had lost its significance, then revived by Zoroastrians in the 20th century.

Sasanian: A major Iranian dynasty that ruled over Iran from the 3rd to the 7th century AD.

Scythians: Indo-Iranian nomadic tribes, they occupied an area extending from European Russia to northern China.

Shahnameh: The book of the kings, Shahnameh is an icon by itself, and is a translation of pre-Islamic stories and myths, and contains the popular history of Iranians before Islam. Written in New Persian in the 10th century AD, its writer Firdowsi, declared, that by writing Shahnameh he saved the Persian language.

Simorg: A legendary mythical bird, popular since the Sasanian era in Iran. Its origin goes back to the Zoroastrian mythology. Its depiction varies over the centuries.

Sistan: Home to the ancient Iranian tribe, Sarangians or Drangians, it occupied modern Sistan in eastern Iran. Under the Greek occupation, the Sacae nomadic tribes of Central Asia invaded it constantly, and eventually gave their name Sacastane (Sistan) to the region.

Sogdiana: In modern day Uzbekistan, Sogdiana was part of the ancient Persian Empire beginning in the 6th century BC. Their language is a branch of the eastern Middle Iranian languages.

Suri Festival: *Suri* means red and the festival was dedicated to the spirits of the dead ancestors. Modern Iranians celebrate it on the last Wednesday of the year by jumping over fires.

Tabari: An Iranian group inhabiting the ancient province of Tabaristan in northern Iran.

Yalda Festival (Shab i Cheleh Festival): Yalda means "birth" and the festival is a celebration of winter solstice on the longest night of the year. It is Zoroastrian in origin. Some of its rituals are similar to Halloween. It is celebrated by all Iranians.

Ziggurat: Ancient temples popular in Mesopotamia, built as huge stepped structures.

Zoroaster: Ancient Iranian prophet, religious reformer and founder of Zoroastrianism. He is believed to have lived around 1100 BC.

Zoroastrians: Followers of the ancient Iranian prophet. Currently there are less than 200,000 Zoroastrians left. Most live in India, Iran, North America and Europe. Their scripture is amongst the world's most ancient that has survived.

Shapur III and Shapur II

Index

Ancient tools for sewing cloth and spinning yarn (3000 - 1000 BC)

Acknowledgements

The publisher would like to thank:

The Iranian Cultural Foundation for permitting the photographing of objects at various museums in Tehran; Mr. Esfandiar Rahim-Mashaei, Head of Iran's Cultural Heritage; Mr. Mehrandish, Director, The National Museum of Iran; Mr Karagar, former Director, The National Museum of Iran; Mrs. Motamedi, former Executive Assistant to Director, The National Museum of Iran; Mr. Vakili, The National Museum of Iran; Mrs. Ahmadi, Director, Reza Abbasi Museum, Tehran; Gulestan and Abgineh Museums in Tehran; Hermitage Museum; Betsy Kohut, Rights and Reproductions, Freer Gallery of Art and Arthur M. Sackler Gallery, Washington D.C.; Dr. Elena Stolyarik, Collections Manager, The American Numismatic Society; Dr. Daniel C. Waugh, Department of History, University of Washington; Joachim and Zohreh Waibel, Vancouver and Art Resource, New York, representing: the Metropolitan Museum of Art, New York; Victoria & Albert Museum, London; Issac Einborn Collection, Tel Aviv; Louvre Museum, Paris; British Museum, London; Berlin Museum, Berlin; Archealogical Museum of Iraq, Baghdad and National Archealogical Museum, Naples.

The publisher would also like to thank Amid Naeini and Joachim and Zohreh Waibel for their generous sponsorship of the project, Dr. Gholamhossein Motamedi for his unconditional support, Shahrezad Moshaver for her help and organizational skills, Parviz Tanavoli, Elham Puriamehr and Sheereen Price for administrative support.

Art Direction
Houman Sadr
Babak Manavi

Picture Credit
Houman Sadr, Davood Sadeghsa,
Joachim Waibel,
Afrooz Nasersharif and Arash Mirlohi.

Illustration
Eliya Tahamtani

Cover Design
Babak Manavi